# In the Heart of the Temple

# ～ In the ～
# Heart of the Temple

*My Spiritual Vision for Today's World*

## Joan Chittister

**BlueBridge**

*Cover design by Cynthia Dunne*
*Cover image by Art Resource, New York*

Library of Congress Cataloging-in-Publication Data
Chittister, Joan.
In the heart of the temple : my spiritual vision for
today's world / Joan Chittister.— 1st ed.
p. cm.
ISBN 0-9742405-1-6
1. Spiritual life—Catholic Church.  I. Title.

BX2350.3.C44 2004
248.4'82—dc22                                    2004016082

Published by
B l u e B r i d g e
An imprint of
United Tribes Media Inc.
240 West 35th Street, Suite 500
New York, NY 10001
www.bluebridgebooks.com

Benetvision
355 East Ninth Street
Erie, PA 16503-1107
www.benetvision.org

Printed in the United States of America
10  9  8  7  6  5  4  3  2

*For Marlene,*
*friend and editor,*
*who has done much over the years*
*both to sharpen this vision*
*and to make it real.*

# Contents

# Foreword

$I$ cherish the inscription that Joan Chittister wrote in a book a score of years ago. She greeted me as an "invisible colleague" but an "effective presence" despite our having had to work together "at distance," a presence still, because "our ideas bind."

That inscription was in *Faith and Ferment* (copublished in 1983 by Augsburg Publishing House and Liturgical Press), to which she contributed 150 pages and I contributed 100. To have two publishers, one Lutheran and one Roman Catholic, connect a Benedictine nun with a Lutheran minister to produce a book together was not a run-of-the-mill venture then, even twenty years after the Second Vatican Council had begun. To have us comment from diverse viewpoints on the same data, while we had not yet met (hence, the "invisible"), was a chance the publishers and the editor, Robert S. Bilheimer, took.

After the book appeared—it was a reflection on data collected in Minnesota, in what was the most ambitious statewide survey of religious attitudes and practices undertaken at that time—I commented lightheartedly to friends that our different vantages showed. Joan would look at data that showed such-and-such a low

percentage of Minnesotans living by this or that biblical mandate, or she would perceive how wanly they exemplified a gospel
promise, and be disappointed if not critical. I would look at the
same data and be surprised and cheered to find that anyone at all
in that secular time believed astonishingly Christian things and
lived out some basic elements of the Christian life. My explanation: she was a religious, fired with enthusiasm for biblical justice
and love, who expected Christians to fly. I had been a parish pastor (at a good parish, I must say), who saw so much of human
nature in its complexity that I was awed if someone made it an
eighth of an inch off the ground.

Since that time I have watched Joan Chittister rise above dis-
appointment and speak of hope, remaining critical but turning
her criticism into transcendent constructive ends. We still are almost "invisible" to each other, though I listen in whenever I can
and read all the time what she issues and how she acts on her
commitments. And I have spoken at conferences where she has
been one of the earlier speakers and find her, as always, a hard act
to follow—but a blessed one.

~

*In the Heart of the Temple* is a collection of her essays, a "Best of
Joan" book in the mode of CDs such as the "Best of Bach." It is
hard to make all the cases she would make in the short span of
essays, but they are all rooted in lifelong study, devotion, and
agency, and thus this collection shows coherence and has force.

What stands out in this book?

First, Joan Chittister is Catholic. I mean *really* Catholic—she
is "of the Roman obedience." Obedience for her never means stu-
pefying submission to what leadership in the church-of-the-
moment propounds and enforces, but willing assent to what Christ
established, governs, prods, and blesses through his collegial body.
And "Catholic" for her means that the faith penetrates the whole
(*kata=holos*) of reality, and quickens the whole creation. With that
wider sweep she embraces those of us who are catholic but not
Roman Catholic.

Second, she is religious. Creatively restless in community, she cannot conceive of her life fulfilled apart from community, even when occasions call her to be distant. She never finds the community "invisible." When I looked through my copy of *Faith and Ferment* while writing this foreword, I found tucked inside a review of it by Kenneth Woodward in *Newsweek* (September 19, 1983). He quoted Joan and me as having discerned and coined the concept of "'pick-and-choose' Christianity" "in which individuals take what they want from church tradition and pass over what does not fit their own spiritual goals." (Thanks to an American speechwriter, that phrase started working its way into the papal vocabulary, and John Paul II used it chidingly on an American trip. Happily, we had not copyrighted the phrase.) Joan Chittister stands in the tradition, takes from it, shakes it up, rattles it around, finds new meanings in it, but does not throw it away. She is a thinker in tradition and "in community."

Third, to the core, she is Benedictine. She lives by the Rule, cherishes the ethos, and embodies what to some of us seems to be near the heart of Benedictinism: the welcoming, hospitable spirit. She lets all of us guests, her readers, "be received as Christ."

Joan Chittister persuades, in the best sense of that term, and does not preach, in the worst sense of that one. She is pastoral. But being pastoral does not mean being soft. The late Cardinal Bernardin once told me that "his" priests wanted him to be pastoral, by which he thought they meant he should be sentimental and should always go easy on them. No, shepherds—pastors— lead flocks, often at the edge of cliffs where they need to use firm measures. Joan Chittister's moral sense evokes moral judgment, but never from a position that would suggest that she has everything worked out and that she stands above the crowd or apart from the flock.

In addition, *In the Heart of the Temple* reveals Joan to be a stylist. In most essays she takes a saying, an anecdote, a bit of data, a turned phrase, and elaborates on it, using it in each case to support the basic themes so well captured in her one-word chapter titles. And she turns phrases herself. I marked many. This one (see page 136) is typical: As she speaks of reformer Martin Luther, Catherine of Siena, Dorothy Day, and Thomas Merton, she comments: "They did not question because they did not believe what the church taught; they questioned because they did." So does she.

Joan Chittister can be angry, but never in uncontrolled or petty ways. One thinks of Robert Browning's Dante, who "loved well because he hated well," hating whatever stood in the way of the path of love. She focuses her anger into positive channels. One has the feeling from reading this book that if one belongs to a group or caste that she criticizes, and thus you have been criticized, she'd be the first to invite you to breakfast the next morning: no hard feelings.

And she deals simply with complexity, as the very first chapter here, on "Simplicity," suggests. She ponders how to square the way of life she must live and gets to live to advance her gospel cause—jets, good hotels, and all—with the need economically to address human need. The last person Joan lets off the hook is she herself. But there is no trace of self-loathing, self-pity, or narcissistic and over-scrupulous confession here: there is too much to be thought about, addressed, served, or delighted by for her to need to resolve everything before acting or commending a course to others.

In those cases when I get to a seminar, workshop, colloquium, or conference where Joan Chittister has spoken a few hours, or days, earlier, the greeting is constantly this: "You should have heard her!" I often do. And, thanks to dissemination through our print media, *you* can hear her, with her steady voice whose tone translates so well into book form. You *get* to hear her!

Martin E. Marty
Fairfax M. Cone Distinguished Service Professor Emeritus
The University of Chicago

# The Heart of the Temple Lies beyond It

~

M any years ago, I had gone into what I thought was the heart of the temple, the point at which the spiritual life was to become full, become real. I was young, in wonder, drawn by the magnetism of it but totally unconscious of what the magnetism, if I allowed it to draw me into the depth of it, would really demand. At that stage of my spiritual development, it was the trappings of the temple, not really the heart of it, that captivated me. The candles soothed my soul. The chant calmed my spirit. The stained-glass windows and familiar shrines and unending rounds of ritual steadied my sense of spiritual direction. What more could there possibly be to the spiritual life than fidelity to the tradition, regularity in its forms, orderliness in its practices?

I thought that simply being there, in the midst of the message, at the core of the call in the temple was all that constituted living the call. More than that, I thought that the temple itself embodied the whole of what it meant to be holy.

Yet the truth is that I often found religion to be a disconcerting if not a discouraging experience. Good and decent people I knew—divorced women, often abused and battered, who had married again; the gay cousin who had spent his life taking care of his mother; non-churchgoing in-laws; committed activists; friends of various ethnic backgrounds—were standing suspect outside the gates of too many temples. Including my own.

I myself had entered a monastery intent on finding what, I learned later, earlier seekers had called "spiritual consolations." I wanted to "find God." I wanted to be "holy." I wanted to "get to heaven." Most of all, I wanted to feel good about the state of my soul. I wanted a life that was separate from the world, apart from the fray, above the grimy reality of the begging lepers and threatening strangers and bold women and grubby outcasts who populated the Gospels. Surely a monastic life was the way to do that quickly.

But it didn't work.

I began to discover that monastic life itself was basically a routine of good practices designed to open us to the possibility of finding God. But it did not guarantee it. It was all about possibility, not promise. It was not a sure trick or a quick fix. It was, at best, only the means, not the end.

So, as the years went by, I found myself in the kind of confusion which, I came later to understand, makes the spiritual real. The temple preached a message I did not yet see—even in the temple itself:

In a country full of temples the hungry among us were still starving. Too many children were sick and uneducated. The poor were dying without care.

Even the temples themselves had no room for half of creation. Women were never accepted as full members, were always invisible, were forever dismissed—as useless but useful, a kind of heavenly mistake, functional, of course, but not fully human. In many temples, blacks were segregated and homosexuals were chastised, and those the temples called "sinful" were shunned.

Obedience had become the central virtue; law was whatever the system defined. And all the while holy disobedience was what was really needed.

In a country we called "Christian," the Jesus story had become more fancy than fact.

⁓

Then, in the 1960s, the Second Vatican Council and its aftermath called the church, the whole people of God, even the keepers of the temple, to a cataclysmic examination of conscience. From inside the temple, and because of the temple, my whole life was put in question:

What to make of simplicity in an increasingly complex world?

What to make of work in a society driven by profit margins, exploitation, and workaholism?

What to make of the Sabbath in a society cherishing the convenience of 24/7?

Was the stewardship for the earth, as Benedict had envisioned it in the Rule and monasteries had practiced it for centuries, still of use in a time of energy waste and environmental disasters?

Was contemplation a kind of holy uselessness, an escape from reality, in a world that rewarded the driven and the demanding? Were contemplatives only religious charlatans, haunting the world while the rest of society really lived in it?

Were my prayers all these years simply attempting to coax a narcissistic God to do my bidding?

What about empowerment in an environment that was hoarding power like gold, imposing it like thunder? Was power really always to be bowed to, never to be contested? And what was its connection to spirituality?

What about prophecy, what about the prophets? Were they more myth than message, anachronisms left over from more heroic—more gullible—times, or indeed a challenge to our very souls, our own society, myself here and now?

What about wholeness? Was it about getting it all or about refusing it all?

And does sanctity really exist anymore, or it is simply the pious recollection of strange people from an even stranger age?

Has tradition been lost with reform and, if it has, what happens to the soul-centeredness of the person who dares to question it?

Can there truly be equality, the daily acceptance of the other? Can we truly follow the ministries of Jesus—Jesus who walked from Galilee to Jerusalem "doing good" and facing death for it? What do equality and ministry have to do with vision?

Most of all, what does vision have to do with the discipleship of equals and with conversion? With real conversion? With turning away from the nothingness of the empty life to the very fullness of a life that is more spiritual than spiritualized?

Suddenly, the new institutional examination of conscience made sense. All of life had erupted in one great burst of understanding that no amount of regularity and order could possibly bring. There was a world out there that was itself "the heart of the temple." It was now a matter of bringing the temple to the world and the world to the heart of it. But the transition between the two was a walk through spiritual chaos. How could we possibly bring the spiritual truths of one age to bear on the challenges of another?

⟋

"Chaos often breeds life," Henry Brooks Adams wrote, "when order breeds habit." There is a truth to that insight that only makes the spiritual life all the more meaningful, even while making it all the more troublesome.

The truth is that only when disorder erupts do we sometimes see what we have falsely accepted for much too long. Then, shaken out of our complacency, we begin to ask the questions that can lead to a new vision, to conversion, to understanding, to new life.

Paralysis, I am convinced, is as true of the spiritual life as it is of life at large. Spirituality can go flat, too. Bland can set in with a vengeance, calling itself contemplation, blinding us to our own complacency. Spiritual formulas can become a substitute for spiritual sensibilities, spiritual programs a placebo for spiritual growth.

Spiritual practices themselves can begin to trump the spiritual life.

What started out as a genuine search for the God of life can end up over time regularized to the point of rigidity. Then God becomes a distant icon, a kind of holy card figure from whom we expect favors, but to whom we give little actual thought in every-day life. The awareness of God becomes a special category of life rather than life itself. Most of all, the fervor that first led us to search for deeper meaning in life, for purer depths of soul, becomes at best a dim and distant memory. Once the spiritual life has settled down into a kind of comfortable routine, we cease to see what there is around us that is crying out for the thunderous truth of the spiritual:

The government churns out weapon after weapon in peacetime. But we often ignore the connection between that and the peace we seek in our own spiritual life.

The poor sleep on the steps of our temples, and eat in our soup kitchens. But we often do not address the relationship between that and our own spiritual nourishment.

Whole segments of society find themselves denied their civil rights publicly. Women and minorities are looked down on socially. But we often fail to understand that the oppression of any human being is a spiritual issue.

Children and old people, fetuses and the fatally ill, the sick and the handicapped are considered valueless in a society that prizes rugged individualism above all else. But we often do not see the relevance of those false values as they relate to our own spiritual growth.

We do not realize that prayer and prophecy must be one, that Sabbath and stewardship are the same thing, that contemplation and ministry are merely opposite sides of the same immersion in the God-life that we profess to follow in our temple services.

⁓

The spiritual life, the spiritual vision that emerges in this book, is a spirituality of both action *and* contemplation, a spirituality of co-creative contemplation. It requires us both to see what is going on in the world around us and to do everything we can to square it with the will of a loving God for the world that God created. It is deeply immersed in the bond between what is and what should be. It cries to heaven for the realization that the spiritual life depends on the spending of the self to bring the reign of God here and now, always and forever. It is an anthem of personal responsibility for the spiritual quality of the world around us. It is a call to link the heart and the temple.

Where the person of spirit is, the world becomes a spiritual place. To be in the heart of the temple without being in the heart of the world as well is at most only half a spiritual life—because the heart of the temple truly lies beyond it.

That is my spiritual vision for today's world.

Joan Chittister
June 2004

# Simplicity

G regorian chant is playing softly on the small CD player in my office. The house is quiet. The fireplace is lit. It is, at the very least, a charming and bucolic scene. The question is, Is it in any way a study in simplicity of life? In fact, does anything really qualify as a demonstration of simplicity of life anymore? After all, fireplace and silence notwithstanding, I spent an hour on the phone this morning trying to arm wrestle into compliance the little three-pound computer on which I am now writing this article. Then, on Friday of this week I will cross the Atlantic Ocean to do a lecture tour with the same kind of ease I used to feel in going from the back door of our priory across the parking lot to the tiny rural school in which I taught double grades. Is that simplicity of life or isn't it?

And I'm not the only one with the problem: The UPS man tells me that carrying packages is a pretty involved operation these days with computer programs and delivery routes that crisscross the globe. Opening a garage door is a technological process now. Telephone operators don't answer telephones anymore; machines do. Then they connect you to another machine—and this one with a recorded message. No doubt about it: pencils are museum pieces; horses are for show; home is a movable feast, and getting to work has become a two-hour commute.

Yet the subject of the simple life never goes away. Poets tout the virtue of simplicity. Philosophers plumb it. Writers wax sad and serious about its glory, its necessity, its loss, its value, its virtue, its utter sabotage in modern life. Simplicity, it seems, has escaped us. Simplicity, it appears, is gone forever from a global, technological, mobile, and massified world. I suppose I should feel discouraged at even the thought of trying to deal with such an elusive subject. The fact of the matter is, however, that I'm not. If anything, I'm less sure than ever that what we have called simplicity has ever really been simplicity at all. Not in the spiritual sense of the word, not in the way the ancients used it, at least. G. C. Lichtenberg wrote, "The noble simplicity in the works of nature only too often originates in the noble shortsightedness of those who observe it." Simplicity doesn't really exist, in other words. We make it up. It's a sobering thought. We kid ourselves, Lichtenberg implies, and scientists now confirm, when we assume that simplicity is simply an arrangement of indivisible parts of anything. There is absolutely nothing in nature which, by that definition, is truly simple. A one-celled organism is made up of atoms and molecules beyond count and all in intricate relationship to one another. Everything created consorts with something else and depends on it and is held in being by a system that is infinitely sophisticated, interminably complex. The fact is that life is not simple. The fact is that we must learn to deal with our complexities with simplicity.

So, are we chasing a theological rainbow, a poet's fantasy, an adolescent's dream of life without burden, life without stress when we even dare to talk about simplicity of life? No, I don't think so. We may, however, be chasing a vacuum when what we really need is substance.

The hard truth may be that simplicity of life is not necessarily life without things and days without fringe at all. In fact, life without necessities—grueling, unfair, and involuntary poverty—

is not simplicity at all. Life without its essentials is, in fact, social obscenity, a moral responsibility that is incumbent on society at large. No, simplicity may far more properly be life without clutter, life without compulsions, life without a need to control, life that is committed to contemplative vision, whatever ebb, wherever its flow, than it is life without things. Simplicity of life may better these days be what the late Madeleva Wolff, poet and college president, called "the habitually relaxed grasp" than it is life without a collection of gadgets that we never really wanted or needed anyway.

Simplicity of life may simply be more the ability to handle with single-minded unity of soul what life brings than it is to refuse to accept anything except what we are willing to accept on our own terms, sparse and basic as these may be. When rigid vegetarians, for instance, put other people under a great deal of strain cooking for them, I can't help but wonder how really simple that is. When people keep their own offices immaculate by leaving their personal debris in lounges and foyers and public recreation rooms, the question persists: Is that simplicity of life? I see people who handle their own schedules very well because they simply refuse to have their personal priorities interrupted by anybody else's needs. Everybody else is forced to bend to suit them—and so everybody else's lives end up more and more intricate, involved, difficult as a result. So who is really practicing simplicity of life in these cases: The people with controlled menus, controlled physical environments, and controlled schedules or the people whose own lives are twisted and stretched to make that kind of simplicity possible? Simplicity, I am convinced, is far more than having life on our own terms whatever its effect on others.

Simplicity of life in a complex and complicated world is marked, I think, by four characteristics: A life is simple if it is honest, if it is unencumbered, if it is open to a consciousness not its own, if it is serene in the midst of a mindless momentum that verges on the chaotic.

Of all those things, however, honesty is surely its bedrock, its touchstone. We live a simple life when we do not pretend to be something we are not. The graduate of a two-year associate degree program whose simplicity is sincere, for instance, does not affect an Ivy League background. The woman who works in a middle-class office does not feel compelled to buy her worth by spending every available penny on boutique dresses. The financially secure do not live in a maze of conspicuous consumption, buying simply because they can buy, heaping layer upon layer of things over the innards of their unsatiated souls. The truly simple person, in other words, lives a life that is perfectly at ease with itself, that is not seduced by titles and pedigrees, by masks and patinas designed to protect us from the truth about ourselves, to remove us from our origins, to save us from the consequences of our humanity. They do not need to drip with jewelry or cosmetics or clothes to hide their looks or know their worth or feel the value of their own presence.

Truly simple people live with dignity whatever life brings to them. For them, then, only the truth about themselves, pure and unadulterated, really counts. In a society that thrives on image and advertising copy and status it is one thing to equate simplicity with things; it is another thing entirely to remember where you came from at all times, whatever the status you have now achieved—and never to cut the cord. Simplicity has something to do with being willing to have it known that you are from Bethlehem rather than from Beverly Hills.

At base, then, simplicity of life has a great deal more to do with authenticity than it does with things, or else it would be a virtue only for those who had things to forego. Then simplicity would have more to do with classism, with a kind of social play called "voluntary simplicity," than with an attitude of mind that lets us stand in the midst of our worlds naked and unafraid, sure of soul and unencumbered by the seductiveness of the unnecessary and the cosmetic. It would have more to do with accounting than with what the ancients called "purity of heart," that single-minded search for the essence of life rather than for a grasping after its frills, whatever shape those might take in our various worlds.

If one of the major aspects of simplicity in a highly cosmeticized world is honesty, however, the second characteristic must just as surely be detachment. It is one thing to know who we are. It is another thing to be indifferent even to that. Today I have money and a job and a title. On some surprising day, I will not have even that. When that day comes, all the simplicity I have effected will be tested to the core. On that day, I will discover the hard truth that simplicity of life is not frugality of life; it is life unencumbered, life free of the things we own so that they do not own us.

"We own only what cannot be lost in a shipwreck," the Arab proverb teaches. The image is a startling one only because it's true. Yet, no more difficult lesson is ever learned. In a consumer society that depends for its very economic base on the creation of false needs, the very thought of not wanting more than we have becomes an economic heresy. The truth is that if we don't buy, people don't work and so the process never ends. We create what we do not need in order to keep our basic needs at bay. There is very little new in new cars, for instance, but the placement and design of the old gadgets. Clothes don't change, styles do. Stoves and refrigerators, kitchen utensils and bathroom fixtures aren't different from year to year, they're simply painted other colors. It is a miserable cycle of ever-accelerating wants fed by layer after layer of arguments without substance.

But who can stand the thought of winding up behind the times? So, we "keep up," and we accumulate, and we die under the detritus of our own lives. Every person in the house owns a bike, just in case all the bikes might someday, maybe, ever be wanted at once. We keep five pair of scissors because one pair is new and the other four pair—all slightly different, none of them different at all—are still too good to throw away. We keep a dozen nonmatching water glasses for a house of three people. "Just in case; just in case; just in case," we tell ourselves.

The cupboards fill up; the rooms fill up; the basement fills up; the attic fills up with things we never, ever—not even once a year—need, hardly use, or don't know what to do with now that we have them. Is that simplicity? Or is simplicity more the ability to get rid of what we're not using rather than hoarding what we will never touch again? It is easier to fantasize life in a cabin splitting wood than it is to give away the old hammers we own when we buy new ones. And yet whole segments of our population lack even one of all the things we replace so casually. The Arabs have it right. Whatever we now own is simply temporary. We're not taking it anywhere, so what is keeping us from being willing to get rid of it now except, perhaps, the fear that real simplicity is an excursion into trust too demanding of soul to bear?

To face society unfeigned and to walk through the world with hands and hearts unencumbered frees a person for the basics of life. Freedom is the real purpose, the real essence of simplicity. We have insulated ourselves against life to such an extent that we can go for years without living it. Riding around in fine cars everywhere makes it impossible for us to feel the grass that breaks between the cracks of old sidewalks. Musak and Surround-Sound and stereo systems vented from basement to bathroom make it impossible for us to ever appreciate silence. Television saves us from talking to the people we live with for years. Simplicity, on the other hand, is openness to the beauty of the present, whatever its shape, whatever its lack. Simplicity, clearly, leads to freedom of soul. When we cease to be consumed by the need for what we can do without, when we cultivate a sense of enoughness, when we learn to enjoy things for their own sakes, when we learn to be gentle even with what is lacking in ourselves, we find ourselves free to be where we are and to stop mourning where we are not. We find that simplicity is an antidote to depression. The desert monastics tell a story that soothes the soul and saves the sincere heart from legalized simplicity. "Abbot Mark," the tales tell, once said to Abbot Arsenius, "It is good, is it not, to have nothing in our cell that just gives us pleasure? For example, I once knew a brother who had a little wildflower that came up in his cell and he pulled it out by the roots." "Well," said Abbot Arsenius, "that is all right. But each person should act according to her own spiritual way. And if one were not able to get along without the flower, she should plant it again." Simplicity is not the arithmetic of the soul. Simplicity of life is not really about things at all. Simplicity is about being able to take them—and to leave them.

Finally, simplicity of life manifests itself in perfect serenity. The simple person pays close attention to the agitations that eat at the heart. It is our agitations that tell us where life has gone astray for us, has become unbearably complex and eternally confused. If we lack simplicity, if we fret at every delay, become miserable at every change of plans, become miffed at every imagined slight, become irritated at every lapse of deference, become despondent over every lack of gadget, then God has been replaced in us by a god of our own making. Then the simple life, the sanctity of the present moment, the contemplation of the divine in the mundane, the "purity of heart" that centers us on the eternal that is in the now, disappears into oblivion. Then simplicity of heart becomes counterfeit. Chop all the wood you want, give away all the clothes you own, romanticize the praises of the pioneer life, but simplicity has flown you by. There is simply no simplicity in a heart full of agitation, in a soul too distracted by a plethora of projects and products to recognize the One who is among us yet, but invisible in chaos.

No doubt about it, simplicity and serenity carry overtones of the same chord. Both of them ring of an imperturbability that comes from being rooted in a world beyond ourselves where the God who is Everything waits for us to find life at the center beyond the clutter of the commonplace, beneath the chimera of the image, behind the things that pass for God.

Simplicity and serenity, simplicity and honesty, simplicity and openness, simplicity and acceptance are synonyms too long kept secret. But without them simplicity itself is subterfuge.

"Seek God and not where God lives," the desert monastics taught. The lesson is an important one. We cannot play at finding God; we cannot play at life. We must live both unceasingly, intensely, consciously. We must come to see the world around us with the eye of God and respond to it with a compassionate heart. We must be single-minded about the purpose of life, stripped of its non-essentials, set on eternity and sighted by a single eye. The fact is that quiet days, soft music, and nice fires may nourish a simplicity within us, but if we can't deal with the arm-wrestling match that is life—honestly, openly, freely, and serenely—then simplicity of life has escaped us yet. Life as it is, not life as we contrive it and wrench it and want it and demand it, no matter how good we define our wants to be, is the raw material of simplicity. Indeed, "Seek God," the ancients taught, "and not where God lives." Not where we say God lives.

# Work

⁓

Once upon a time, the ancients tell us, a disciple said to the rabbi, "God took six days to create the world and it is not perfect. How is that possible?" "Could you have done better?" the rabbi asked. "Yes, I think I could have," the disciple said. "Then what are you waiting for?" the rabbi said. "Go ahead. Start working."

The story raises three questions about the nature and place of work in life that plague humankind yet: Is work a human punishment for sin or an opportunity to grow in the spiritual life? Is work something to be avoided or something to be embraced? Is work the opposite side of the spiritual life or the ground of the spiritual life?

They are important questions.

If work is meant to be a punishment, then managing to get out of it must be the ultimate sign of spiritual development and God's blessing.

If work is one of life's unfortunate burdens, then work is to be avoided so that life can be lived well and perpetual leisure is a state of life to be striven for.

If work is the enemy of the spiritual life, then people whose lives are full of children and business and the struggle to make ends meet are condemned to spiritual infancy or, at most, to the theology of good intentions: the notion that a person can be saved even if they are too busy to pray. But they can never come to real holiness that way.

The fact of the matter is, however, that most Americans, according to a survey of the Center for Ethics and Corporate Policy, believe that their work is very important to their spirituality and they want a great deal more guidance about the integration of work with their faith life than they say they are now getting from their churches and synagogues—Protestant, Catholic, or Jewish.

And they have good reason to think that way.

Scripture is very clear about the place of work in human life. Human beings were put into the Garden, the Book of Genesis teaches us, "to till it and to keep it." Paradise was not a place for social parasites, in other words. Adam and Eve, it is clear, were expected to take care of what they had been given. The Garden of Eden was not an episode in irresponsibility. The Garden of Eden was a place for creativity and commitment, for accountability and constructive action, for maintaining the fruits and guarding the legacy of their lives for generations to come.

No doubt about it: It is sin that made what we were meant to do more difficult to do. What was meant to be easy we must now, thanks to sin, do "by the sweat of our brow." But sin is not the reason we are doing it. On the contrary. Sin disrupted the vision, true. We are often confused about what we should be doing in life. Sin muddied the way, yes. We are often conflicted about how to go about a good thing. Sin broke the relationships that make work personally satisfying and socially valuable, indeed. We too often fight among ourselves now for profit and lose a sense of the purpose of the work. But sin is not the reason we work.

Genesis is explicit: We work to complete the work of God in the world. Work, then, may be the most sanctifying thing we do.

The question is, What does that mean to us today in our time and here in our country and now in our homes?

Two poles compete for contemporary attention when people

talk about work: One pole is workaholism; the other pole, pseudo-contemplation.

The workaholic can use work as a substitute for other things in life. Work can be a way to avoid a carping husband or a dull and loveless wife. Work can save us from the noise of the children or the consciousness of the bills. Work can be a shield from having to do anything else in life. Work can be what guards us from having to make conversation or spend time at home or broaden our social skills. Work can simply satisfy the compulsion to make money, money, and more money. And that kind of work is a deep psychic torture, a Plexiglas between work and life, an external antidote to a sense of internal emptiness.

Or, workaholics can become their work. If it is valued, they are valuable. If it fails, their entire life has failed. Workaholics identify with what they do, and when what they do is over—when they get sick or retire or lose a job—they are over, too. Their sense of self is over. Their joy in life is over. Their very reason for existence is over. It is a sad distortion of the will of God for human work, a tragic end to an exciting possibility.

On the other hand, the thirst for pseudo-contemplation is just as sad. To assume that life is for lounging and then to blame that kind of injustice to others on the search for God is to make a mockery of the public life of Jesus. When we were young novices, in fact, the novice mistress was quite explicit. None of us were allowed to go to chapel between prayer times. The message was quite clear, even in a monastery: Sloth is not a Christian virtue. Holy leisure was not a license to live irresponsibly. Co-creation is a mandate writ deep in the human heart. Work itself is holy.

But why and how?

Western culture has not treated work kindly. We have a history of serfs who worked like slaves and sweatshops that robbed people of their human dignity and basic rights. We have lived in a capitalism that bred brutal competition and unequal distribution of goods as well as inventiveness and profit. We are watching the poor get poorer even while they are working. We see the rich get richer even when they don't. And we realize that the middle class must work harder every year just to stay where they were last year. What can possibly be good about all of that? That depends on the work we do and why we're doing it.

In the first place, work is what we do to continue what God wanted done. Work is meant to be co-creative. Keeping a home that is beautiful and ordered and spiritually nourishing and artistic is co-creative. Working in a machine shop that makes gears for tractors is co-creative. Working in an office that processes loan applications for people who are themselves trying to make life more humane is co-creative. Working on a science project, on the other hand, whose sole intent is to destroy life makes a mockery of creation. To say that science is blind, that science is objective, that science is neutral when what you make is napalm and the components of germ warfare and plutonium trigger-fingers is to raise ethical questions of overwhelming proportions.

God the creator goes on creating through us. Consequently, to have a gift that can nourish the community and to let it go to waste because "cooking is woman's work," or "the more you do, the more they want you to do" strikes at the very heart of human community and the process of creation itself. Work, then, is to be done for its own sake, because it is good, because it is needed, because we have the gift for it. Work is not simply a means to make money so that, eventually, we will not have to work at all. Work is what brings us closer to what the kingdom is meant to be. And if our work at making the world a better place fails, have we failed too? "If you expect to see the final results of your work," an Arab proverb teaches, "you have simply not asked a big enough question."

But work is not simply a gift to others. Work develops the worker, as well. Work is the one exercise in gift-giving that always comes back to the giver. The more I work at anything, the better I get at it. And the better I get at something, the better I feel about myself. It is the fear of being good for nothing that destroys people. It is good work well done that gives us the right to say that we are valuable members of the human community.

Finally, work is an exercise in love. Leo Tolstoy, the Russian novelist, wrote once, "The sole purpose of life is to serve humanity." It is what I have cared for that I grow to care about. People who tell you they love you but never do a thing for you, people who say they value the family but never join the family in any project, people who say they care about the planet but never do a thing to make the planet a more human place to live, fail to see that life is a venture in human development and that work is its key.

Work makes time worthwhile. Time is all we have to make our lives bright-colored, warm, and rich. Time spent on an artificial high is time doomed to failure. Time spent amassing what I cannot possibly use is time wasted. Time spent in gray, dry aimlessness is a prison of the thickest walls. But good work that leaves the world softer and fuller and better than even before is the stuff of which human satisfaction and spiritual value are made. There will come a moment in life when we will have to ask ourselves what we spent our lives on and how life in general was better as a result of it. On that day we will know the sanctifying value of work.

Work has been badly warped, badly misused in our society. The globalization of industry is being used to bring people into a new kind of slavery. U.S. corporations are leaving their home soil to manufacture computer parts in Mexico where they pay poor women $5.00 per day to make the boards which they will later sell for $500 at the expense of the working class in both countries.

Success has become more important than value. The drive for success at work, instead of success in life, continues to make people ill and to destroy marriages and to increase the level of personal dissatisfaction.

Efficiency has become a god that will accept the sacrifice of people for the sake of the production line and the profits it promises. We use what will do a thing faster, not necessarily what will do it better. We hire people for profit and retire them in mid-life, without pensions, when they have served their use to the company and then go out and hire the next generation of young and cheap and indefatigable laborers.

Indeed, the sanctity of work must be reclaimed if humanity is ever to be reclaimed in a world wounded and imperiled by sins against the co-creativeness of work. The disassociation that comes from being only one small point of the assembly line of modern life has dulled our consciences and blinded our eyes to our own part in a world where death is our greatest export. The days are gone when the family that tilled the field also planted and harvested it together. Now owners own and planters plant and sprayers spray and pickers pick and sellers sell and none of them take responsibility for the pesticides that reach our tables. Scientists calculate and designers design and welders weld and punchers punch and assemblers assemble and none of them take responsibility for a nuclear world.

The implications of a spirituality of work in a world such as this are clear, it seems: Work is my gift to the world. It is my social fruitfulness. It ties me to my neighbor and binds me to the future.

Work is the way I am saved from total self-centeredness. It gives me a reason to exist that is larger than myself. It makes me part of possibility. It gives me hope. Martin Luther wrote: "If I knew that the world would end tomorrow, I would plant an apple tree today."

Work gives me a place in salvation. It helps redeem the world from sin. It enables creation to go on creating. It brings us all one step closer to what the kingdom is meant to be.

Work is meant to build community. When we work for others, we give ourselves and we can give alms as well. We never work, in other words, for our own good alone.

Work leads to self-fulfillment. It uses the gifts and talents we know we have and it calls on gifts of which we are unaware.

Work is its own asceticism. When we face the work at hand, with all its difficulties and all its rigors and all its repetition and all its irritations and accept it, we do not need to traffic in symbolic penances. What today's work brings is what is really due from me to God. And if we do it well, we will have spiritual discipline aplenty. What's more, when this is not the job we want but we cannot get any other, when this is not the wage we need to make ends meet but they will not pay more, when we see younger workers and more automated machines and job slowdowns begin to encroach on the work we once thought would be our lifetime security, then virtues of faith and simplicity of life and humility come into play in ways too real to be reduced to empty rituals or religious gestures. Then work becomes the raw material of wisdom and holy abandonment.

Finally, work is the way we really live in solidarity with the poor of the world. Work is our commitment not to live off others, not to sponge, not to shirk, not to cheat. Giving less than a day's work for a day's pay, shunting work off onto underlings, assuming that personal days are automatically just additional vacation days, taking thirty-minute coffee breaks in the fifteen-minute schedule, doing one coat of paint where we promised to do two, are not what was meant to "till the Garden and keep it."

Work is our gift to the future. It is our sign that God goes on working in the world through us. It is the very stuff of divine ambition. And it will never be over. The philosopher wrote, "Do you want a test to know if your work in life is over? If you are still alive, it isn't." As the rabbi and the disciple both well knew, God needs us to complete God's work. Now.

# Sabbath

~~~~~

The 20th century may, when the long view of history makes a final assessment, rank as one of the crossover moments in the development of the human race. Two world wars, the institutionalized holocaust of an entire people, the nuclearization of the globe, the dawn of organ transplants, the advent of scientific birth control, the cloning of animals, the wholesale raping of natural resources, and the emergence of the Internet all signal a period of massive change, a reshaping of the human economy. Life-altering situations such as these constitute the before and after moments of a watershed culture. The apex of the Enlightenment ideal for many, they are, at the same time, perceived by others as the ultimate low point of classical philosophy. From one perspective or another, they denote science run rampant or traditional theology under siege. Out of them have come some of the best, and some of the worst, moments in human history.

Indeed, the century brought us both great threat and great possibility. Interestingly enough, though each of these historical moments, and many other moments, as well, depending on who's naming them, may certainly figure in somebody's catalogue of sins or someone else's catechism of progress, the mere branding of these elements and others like them as either good or bad does not necessarily testify to any of them morally. It takes a great deal more than either public approval or personal denouncement to mark anything as certainly moral, amoral, or immoral. It takes reflection. It takes care. It takes criteria to evaluate a thing. It takes reflection and soul. It takes exactly what we may in our time now be missing most: the spirit of Sabbath. One of the cardinal sins of the recent past may well be the loss of Sabbath.

Play we know about and make it big business. Leisure we are committed as a culture to pursuing. The concept of Sabbath, however, simply escapes the modern mind. Despite the fact that the idea of Sabbath is the oldest in the Judeo-Christian tradition, it is, in a culture of cars and planes, of 24-hour-a-day shopping malls and seven-day-a-week services, the lost art of the present.

Scholars of the Talmud tell us that the reason God created Sabbath was not because God needed rest but in order to model rest, to sanctify rest, to demand rest of us so that by regularly resting in God we could ourselves become new people. Sabbath, the tradition says, crowns life with four dimensions.

In the first place, thanks to Sabbath, everyone in the society is equal at least one day a week. On the Sabbath, both rich and poor have the right to live a privileged life exempt from drudgery. Second, Sabbath makes the whole world free. The upper class puts down its burden of administration. The lower class, the slaves, lives free from the demand to take orders. The third gift of Sabbath, the rabbis teach us, is the foretaste of heaven that comes with resting in God, refreshing family life, and internalizing the Word that nourishes our souls for the rest of the week. The fourth blessing of the Sabbath comes from taking the time to consider the purpose of life, to determine if we can say with the Creator about our own work in the world, "That's good." The product I make enhances life and "That's good." The wages I pay enable life and "That's good." The decisions I make bring justice to life and "That's good."

Sabbath, in other words, is meant to enrich life, to measure life, to bring reflection to life, to engender life with soul.

Sabbath is for resting in the God of life and bringing more to life ourselves as a result. Sabbath stays us in mid-course and gives us the opportunity to begin again, week after week after week. If one-seventh of every life is devoted to rest, then we have been given 52 days a year, or over 3,500 days in 70 years, or approximately ten years of Sabbath or rest or reflection in a lifetime—all designed to be used to determine the meaning and substance, the purpose and direction of our lives. Sabbath should be those time-out days when we allow ourselves to look at life in fresh and penetrating ways. Sabbath calls us to worship what deserves to be worshipped and to dismiss from the center of our souls what does not.

But our society has found other things to worship on the Sabbath. We have come to worship consumerism by turning Sundays into some of the biggest shopping days of the year. We have come to worship freedom from family, freedom from worship, freedom from the self. Thinking has become the last thing in the world we want to do on the Sabbath. We have turned thought into human vegetation and called it rest. We have made a desert of the soul and called it re-creation. We have substituted play and leisure for soul-searching and beauty, for intimacy and awareness of the larger things in life. We have created a culture that turns the Sabbath into a race for escape, a passion for things, a collection of distractions, a paean to emptiness.

Indeed, we are a long, long way from Sabbath and so near, so very near, to social dissipation as a result.

We don't stop to think much about anything anymore. We don't stop at all, in fact. Our generation has learned to "multi-task," to "manage" our time. We open our mail while we talk on the telephone. We correct papers or shift computer files while we watch television. We take the kids to play in the park while we sit in the car to finish writing this month's report. We work every day of the week and twice as much on the Sabbath. It's become catch-up time instead of reflection time. We have lost a sense of awareness, of attention, of what the monastics call "mindfulness." No wonder we can come to the brink of human cloning and hardly notice. No wonder we can watch the oppression of half the human race and take it for granted. No wonder we can watch the total unraveling of life in every arena and find little or no time to participate in the public debates that ought to underlie the creation of social consensus before we find ourselves inheriting what we did not desire, acceding to what we cannot morally sustain, bequeathing what we dare not countenance.

When Yahweh created the Sabbath, the specter of thoughtlessness was created as well. Having created the opportunity for awareness, the opportunity for the oblivious was created as well. We unleashed nuclear weapons upon the world and failed to think about the moral implications of that, both then and now. We clawed our way through the rain forests and failed to consider as a people the long-range implications of that for generations to come. We lost a sense of Sabbath and took no notice as a culture of the starvation of soul, the loss of intimacy, and the exhaustion of mind that derived from depriving ourselves of reflection. We turned Sundays into weekdays and wonder what happened to neighbors and nature and our nervous systems.

We multi-task. We buy. We run from ourselves at increasingly greater speeds. Clearly, the sin is not in the science, in the profit, in the play. The sin lies in the loss of the Sabbath mind, the regularly recurring awareness that science and money and play are merely elements of life, not its essence.

The proverb reads, "Now people exploit people. But after the revolution, it will be just the opposite." Without the reawakening of the Sabbath mind, there is no doubt.

# Stewardship

W̶e have, as a people, tried every new trick we know to balance our desire for "the good life" with its effects. We've increased our technology, multiplied our laws, and expanded our educational efforts, but nothing seems to be working. Maybe it's time to try anew what worked well enough to save a civilization centuries before us so that it might save us again.

The fact is that for one set of values—hard work, respect for the land, simplicity, care, and stewardship—our generation has preferred another criteria: profit, consumption, quick returns, short-term gains, and instantaneous gratification. The result, it seems, is a society that is destroying itself at the hands of its own success.

Crops have never grown either so fast or so big in the history of humankind, and yet more people every year starve to death on barren land. Water has never been so conductible and yet so un-usable; it has never been so in demand in all of recorded civilization, and yet the cost of it has never been so high. Travel and the inter-action between peoples have never been so common, and yet peace and security are missing. People have never been employed in larger numbers by major industries in every country of the globe, and yet whole masses of people have never been poorer or less able to sustain themselves.

What we call the "underdeveloped" countries of the world have been supplying natural resources and human labor for the needs and wants of the West for generations now, but never getting richer themselves and never, obviously, getting developed.

The question, of course, is, Why? And the answer is crucial to all of us because this time it is the globe and not the neighborhood or the nation that is at stake.

The Sufi tell a story that may best illustrate the problem, and a very ancient, very modern spirituality gives us a model that may best demonstrate its answer. The Sufi tell the story of a people who were searching for fullness of life: "There are three stages in one's spiritual development," said the Master, "the carnal, the spiritual, and the divine." "Well, Master," the eager disciples asked, "What is the carnal stage?" "That's the stage when trees are seen as trees and mountains as mountains," the Master answered. "And the spiritual?" the disciples continued. "The spiritual is when one looks more deeply into things. Then trees are no longer trees and mountains no longer mountains." "And the divine?" the disciples asked in awe. "Ah, yes, the divine," the Master smiled. "Well, divine enlightenment," the master said and chuckled, "is when trees become trees again and mountains, mountains."

We have a great deal, it seems, to learn from the story ourselves. Even a superficial analysis of the last fifty years, let alone a study of the last two hundred years of shift from an agricultural to an industrial society, is clear proof of a continuing reversal in attitude about the concept of nature and our place in it.

In 1940 if a family bought a living room suite, they expected to own it for life, to move it into their first home, to raise their children on it, to have it be the centerpiece of the house when they were grandparents. People saw trees as trees in those days. If you used one, you planted one. If you shaped one to your own life needs, you honored the life in it and cared for it well and you kept it forever.

Today, living room suites and the trees that go to produce them are thrown away on a regular basis. One tree after another goes down to make new living suites for people who have grown tired of the ones before them. Today, trees are not seen as trees. Today trees and water and air and land have taken on the image of profit for the few, the image of affluence for the others, the image of need for far too many and, tragically, we consider ourselves "advanced" because of it.

In Mexico City, they need clean air but industries consume it with toxic belch at speeds far beyond the power of nature to cleanse itself for another generation, and so the risk of brain damage hangs in every cloud of smog that droops between the mountains.

In Haiti, hillsides are stripped of trees for firewood because the poor have no other source of energy but, because of this practice, the valleys flood out every spring, destroying houses and crops and the lives of other people too poor to lose another thing.

In the Philippines, land of 1,000 islands, the water runs dirty and dangerous from open cesspools and unregulated industrial waste.

Worse, perhaps, than the fact that people are in a great state of natural deprivation and that the planet faces an eroding reservoir of resources is the fact that we have called all the human degradation that went along with such conscienceless profitmaking a sign of God's judgment on the lazy and the feckless and the spiritually immature. God blessed with material good those who were spiritually righteous, the theologians of the industrial revolution claimed. From this point of view, those who lack things lack them primarily because they lack virtue. Goodness, in other words, gives us a claim on God's blessing, and prosperity is a sign of God's favor. All others, the evangelists of capitalism claimed, were full of sin or God would have filled their lack. As a result, we have come to blame the poor for their condition and to see it as no obligation of our own.

And there is lack aplenty. The problem is that it is not the morals of the destitute that must now come under scrutiny. According to Worldwatch Institute (2002), the United States and Europe alone spend 18 billion dollars a year on cosmetics, 17 billion on pet food,

15 billion on perfumes, 14 billion on ocean cruisers, and 11 billion on ice cream just in Europe. That is a total of 75 billion dollars.

But to eliminate hunger and malnutrition around the world would cost 19 billion dollars, universal literacy could be achieved for 5 billion, accessible clean water could be provided for 10 billion, and every child in the third world could be immunized for just over 1 billion dollars. That is a total of 35 billion dollars.

Over 1 billion people, 20% of the world's population, lack reasonable access to safe drinking water, 40% of the people of the world lack basic sanitation facilities and, as droughts brought on by greenhouse gases increase, many millions die from starvation.

Indeed there is something immoral about all of that, but this time it is the policies and stratagems and expenditures of the affluent nations of the world that must be evaluated. If the world that spends millions of dollars every day on instruments of destruction needs security and defense, it is surely food security, air security, and water security that must have priority. Otherwise, generations to come carrying the responsibility to assure the security of their people but afflicted by malnutrition may not be sane enough or rational enough or intelligent enough to do so without harm to others.

It is defense against erosion and defense against energy loss and defense against the ravishment of global resources that are key to national sovereignty and world peace. Like the Sufi disciple we have begun to see other things in the trees and mountains—profit, the good life, consumer goods, production—that we call Divine but which clearly fall far short of fullness of life for everyone. There must be more to the good life than this, we know.

The problem is, Where shall we go to find a model of what it takes to live globally if our own educational system and technological society and legislative policies are not able, apparently, to provide the standards that take us beyond a thirst for things, things, and more things? More than that, What will have to change in our own lives if life is to continue to be lived at a level of decency and beauty and health and possibility and the globe is to be preserved?

The answer, I think, is twofold. First, we must begin to re-examine our theologies of creation. Then we must return to the ideals that saved Europe once and were then abandoned for short-term gain. The answer, I think, lies in the history and values of a way of life devised in the fifth century and dynamic to this day.

Benedictine monasticism was a good gift for bad times. And the fifth century was definitely bad times for Europe. With the breakdown of the Roman Empire, the countryside was in disarray. Roads to market were prowled by thieves, the towns were unguarded and unserviced, vast properties were overrun, peasants were dispossessed, life was unsafe, unpredictable, and undeveloped.

People sat and starved on untilled land or roamed and starved on unkept roadways as they searched for work and food from abandoned town to abandoned town where order was a thing of the past and markets had been long closed. The world of sophisticated cities that had been part of the legacy of Roman roads and Roman law and Roman guards and Roman administration was, for all practical purposes, over. Society had become a parade of rural villages where poor and uneducated people eked out a subsistence existence on dry and hardened land.

It was monasticism that became the economic fly-wheel of the age, the institution that provided a counterweight to chaos.

Benedictine monasticism was designed to be communal, stable, and self-supporting. Unlike other religious figures of the period, monastics did not live solitary lives in desert cells or in woodland hermitages. They did not wander through the countryside begging for alms and food. They were not spiritual athletes whose piety rested on grand feats of fasting and human deprivation.

Benedictine monastics were formed to live a community life centered on God, in peace with all of humankind both within and outside of their own monasteries, and in harmony with nature. "When they live by the labor of their hands," the Rule of Benedict wrote, "as our ancestors and the apostles did, then are they truly monastics" (RB 48:8).

Most important of all, perhaps, was the fact that the monastics themselves were tied to the land. Where their monasteries were is where they themselves would have to make a living for communities that grew rapidly and grew large. Whatever the quality of the land, they would have to till it and enhance it and harvest it and live from it. All over Europe, monastics cleared the forests and put back into cultivation land that had been left barren and sterile by migrating peoples that had allowed it to fall into ruin. One group of monastics, the Cistercians, even preferred to settle in wilderness areas where they cleared the ground and turned whole uninhabitable regions into some of Europe's most fertile farmlands or reforested valleys.

Around these large, stable communities, whose land was expanded yearly both by reclamation projects and the gifts of pious benefactors, grew up villages full of people for whom the monastery became employer, school, spiritual and social center. The monastery itself, then, became the local industry and social axis around which whole societies developed.

Property given to the monasteries, for instance, was seldom attached to the original land grant itself. Instead, the monastery fields, meadows, vineyards, forests, and waters were spread across the continent. There were French monasteries with possessions in the eastern part of the empire, while the monastery of Fulda in Germany held land in Italy. By the year 1100, over two thousand communities were part of the Cluniac system alone, living, working, functioning, holding feudal renters, and producing in like ways all across Europe. As John Henry Newman wrote, Benedictines "were not dreaming sentimentalists, to fall in love with melancholy winds and purling rills and waterfalls and nodding groves. . . ." No, these monks "could plough and reap, . . . hedge and ditch, . . . drain, . . .lop, . . . carpenter, . . . thatch, . . . make hurdles for their huts, . . . make a road, . . . divert or secure the streamlet's bed." And as they approached wilderness after wilderness this way, "the gloom of the forest departed. . . ."

Most of all, each of the monasteries that lived under the Rule of Benedict operated with a vision of work and the land that marked the continent and its peoples for centuries.

The question is, then, What did these people learn from the monasteries that enabled them to salvage a dying continent from decay and misuse that might be good news to our own time?

The answer is that Benedictine monasticism is as much a way of seeing and working and living as it is a way of praying. It is a spiritual vision that affects a person's whole style of life.

The Rule of Benedict does not deal explicitly with the managing of property or the cultivation of land. What the Rule of Benedict is concerned with is the attitude that individuals take to everything in existence. As a result, this way of life has lasted for over 1,500 years and may well be as important to our own generation as it has been in times past.

Why? Because Benedict of Nursia's rule of life for monastics is not based on "taking dominion" over the earth as some readers of the Book of Genesis have emphasized. Benedict's theology of life is clearly based instead on the passage in Genesis that teaches that humanity was put in the Garden "to cultivate it and to care for it."

Benedict requires five qualities of the monastic that affect the way the monastic deals with the things of the earth: praise, humility, stewardship, manual labor, and community, each of them designed to enable creation to go on creating.

Benedictine monasticism roots a person in a community of praise. Monastics are life-positive people whose attitudes are formed by the daily recitation of a psalmody that stresses the splendor of God in nature and the general goodness and connectedness of the cosmos. "Sun and moon, praise God," the monastic prays weekly. "Light and dark, wind and rain, praise God," the psalms go on. "Birds of the air and creatures of the sea, praise God." No gloom-and-doom religion here. In monastic spirituality, everything that is, is good and to be noticed and to be honored and to be reverenced. Nothing is expendable. Nothing is without a value of its own. Nothing is without purpose. Nothing is without beauty and quality and good.

For the holder of a monastic vision of life, then, to take from the land and not to replace it, to destroy it without reclaiming it, to have it without enhancing it is to violate the covenant of life. It was indeed a very monastic thing to replant the forests of Europe and to reclaim the swamps of France and to irrigate the fields of Germany in the Middle Ages. And it is a monastic gift, in an age that destroys with impunity, to recognize the value of everything, to recycle rather than to waste, to conserve energy rather than to pollute, to beautify rather than to distort an environment so that the whole world can come to praise.

Benedictine humility—the notion that we each occupy a place in the universe that is unique but not compelling, wonderful but not controlling—is an antidote to excess in anything and everything. In the Benedictine view of life, monastics are to have what they need and not a single thing more: a small room, the tools of the craft, a balanced diet, plain clothes, good books. The monastic is clearly to receive whatever is necessary. On the other hand, the monastic is to hoard nothing so that others, too, can have the goods of life. "Whenever new clothing is received, the old should be returned at once and stored in a wardrobe for the poor," the Rule reads (RB 55). None of us, in other words, has an exclusive right to the fruits of creation.

It was humility and the sense of place that comes from it that led monastics of the Middle Ages to provide places of refuge for poor pilgrims and to house their noble novices in common spaces and simple cells alongside uneducated peasant monks and simple laboring types. It was humility that led monastics to care for the land rather than simply to live off of it.

In an age that preaches the gospel of rugged individualism and "free-market" capitalism, monastic spirituality is a gift thrown again at the feet of a society made poor for the sake of the oligarchy of the wealthy. Benedictine humility stands with simplicity in the face of greed, conspicuous consumption, and the gorging of two-thirds of the resources of the world by one-third of the people of the world, Europeans and North Americans. The simple fact is that none of us can in conscience consume what belongs by human right to another.

#3 Stewardship is a monastic mindset that fairly riddles the Rule. The monastic is to "care for the goods of the monastery as if they were the vessels of the altar." The abbot is reminded that he will be required "to give an account of his stewardship" of the monastery. "Let him recognize," he is told, "that his goal must be profit for the monastics, not preeminence for himself." The cellarer or manager of the monastery is told to steward the resources of the community "like a father," solicitous for "the sick, children, guests and the poor" (RB 31). Never does monastic life or any part of it exist only for itself and its own profit. What the Benedictine monastic does and has is always for the sake of the other.

In a world where control of resources, control of labor, control of profits, control of markets is the order of the day, monastic ecology calls for the cherishing of the entire planet and all of its peoples.

#4 Manual labor, the actual shaping of our private worlds, is a hallmark of Benedictine monasticism. Every monastic, no matter how learned or how important, is, literally, to take life into his or her own hands by shoveling its mud and planting its seeds and carrying its boulders and digging its wells.

It was manual labor that made the monastic a co-creator of the universe where creation goes on creating daily. When you have washed a floor and fixed a chair and painted a wall and cleared an acre and cleaned a machine, the floor and the chair and the wall and the land and the machine become important to you. You have made yourself responsible for its life.

But responsibility for life is what the modern world has most lost. In a throwaway society, nothing is seen as having life. Things have simply a temporary usefulness. As a result, we have glutted our landfills with styrofoam cups, used once and used half and then discarded to lie unconsumed forever while we bury the human race in its own garbage.

Out of touch now with how long it takes to clean a polluted stream or grow a tree or dissipate a field of smog, we throw bottles overboard in our lakes and waste paper by the ream and allow three people in three cars to drive to the same place day after day after day. We have indeed come a long way from the fields and the kitchens of ages past and live now in cubicles of computers and machines, the effects of which have no meaning to us whatsoever. When a young man pushes the button to detonate a nuclear test, it is because he has lost a sense of the monastic vision of life that comes with working to preserve it with your own hands. When a young woman dumps the half-eaten casserole down a garbage disposal rather than eat leftovers, there is no sense of the monastic vision in her. When a family throws cans and bottles out a car window, it is because they have lost a sense of the value of all things that comes with the manual labor that is essential to the monastic vision of the co-creation of life.

Finally, Benedictine monasticism is rooted in human commu-nity, stable, gifted, equal, and needy. In the monastic community of the fifth century, when slavery was considered a natural part of the human condition, the members of the monastic commu-nity lived as equals, nobles and peasants, learned and illiterate, officials and members, side by side. Only respect for the amount of time spent in monastic life and the new kind of mentality that it formed in a society of violence and exploitation distinguished the place of one monastic from another.

Here in this world where no one was to be considered the servant or the lackey or the colony of the other, everyone had impartial claim on the goods of the community. Only the concept of "enoughness" regulated the distribution of goods in the mo-nastic community. "Whoever needs less should thank God and not be distressed," the Rule instructs, "but whoever needs more should feel humble because of his weakness. . . ." (RB 34). In this society that considered inner riches the wealth to be sought after, the notion of the accumulation of goods as a sign of character weakness was clear.

It is time to see the character weakness in our own patterns of conspicuous consumption and greedy capitalism. It is time to realize that the rest of the globe is not our backyard to dominate. It is our garden "to till and to keep."

It is precisely this monastic sense of praise, humility, stew-

ardship, manual labor and community that taught Europe and fruc-
tified Europe and saved Western civilization. It is those things
that we in our time lack now and to our peril.

Enlightenment for our age, too, as for the Sufi disciples of the
tale, requires that we begin to see trees as trees and mountains as
mountains again, but newly. We must begin to see the planet as
something with a life of its own, holy and filled with the glory of
God. It is not to be exploited by us or discarded by us or used by
us for false and short-term profit. We must begin to see the sa-
credness of life itself, in all its forms, for all peoples of the earth.
We must begin to understand that nature is not separate from us;
it is basic to us. Its fate is our fate. Its future is our future. Its life is
essential to our own.

If we can begin to see differently and to think differently and
to live differently from generations before us then we will be able to
grow enough crops to feed everyone. We will not only be able
to draw water across deserts but we will be able to keep it clean and
clear and healthful. We will have the water we need at reasonable
cost because we will have learned to conserve, not waste it. We
will have the peace and security that comes when people are not
threatened either by famine or futility. We will have a world where
all people are paid just wages for the work of their hands. We will
have a world where being part of an "underdeveloped" nation is a
challenge, not a state of life, not a terminal disease, not an affliction
without hope of cure.

Indeed, if we begin to see with monastic vision we may be
able to save civilization once more. We will see all of life as good
and refuse to dominate and diminish it. We will have the humility
to know our place in the universe and respect, reclaim, and revive
the life around us. We will see ourselves as the stewards of the
planet, not its owners, and we will pass it on to the next generation undamaged. We will work to shape a world full of beauty,
full of possibility. We will build up the human community in such
a way that there are no such things as "undeveloped" peoples.

Thomas Merton wrote once, "You have to take God and creatures all together and see God in creation and creation in God and

don't ever separate them. Then everything manifests God instead of hiding God or being in the way of God as an obstacle." It is the monastic vision that calls us to see the trees and mountains of our own day as part of the glory of God and to treat them accordingly.

# Contemplation

*A*s a young sister, I remember working very hard at prayer. I prepared and prepared for prayer. At that time, our prayer was in Latin. While I wasn't all that bad at Latin, no one really wrestles with the nuances of the spiritual life in another language, let alone a dead one. So, I prepared in English as well. Yet, even though my preparation improved, I couldn't see that anything was happening in my life. I didn't feel closer to God or more aware of God's presence.

Then in the early 1960s I was given a copy of *Abandonment to Divine Providence* by Jean-Pierre De Caussade. He added an element that had been missing for me. It was the concept of the sacrament of the present moment, the notion that what is now is where God is for me now.

The awareness of God's presence had become my greatest value. After that, I began to see that we are steeped in God. But our awareness of this is so limited. I think that's true because we have been trained to pray, instead of being trained in prayer.

When you are trained to pray, you can find yourself in a phenomenal amount of formulas, and the pre–Vatican II church abounded in them. These formulas should have been aids to prayer, but often they became ends in themselves: for example, the nine first Fridays, the so-many Saturdays, the so-many decades of the rosary. These are the things I'm thinking of when I say we were trained to pray. It was a very product-oriented method.

Being trained in prayer, on the other hand, can lead to contemplation. Its starting point is the realization that potentially everyone is a contemplative. Contemplation is there for the taking. All you have to do is give yourself over to it. That means you give yourself not to the prayer, or to the prayer formula, but rather to something beyond the prayer, and that something, of course, is Someone, God.

Contemplatives are people whose consciousness of God permeates their entire lives. Their awareness of God's presence magnetizes them and directs them beyond everything else, beyond all other values. Contemplatives are aware that God creates them, sustains them, and challenges them. As a result, all other values and agendas fall away. I don't mean contemplatives find no value in other things—for example, in a career, or money, or achievement. These things, however, never become their greatest value. The awareness of God's presence remains the greatest value.

In essence, according to all the great mystics, contemplation is, and I think continues to be, this consciousness of living steeped in God, of being surrounded by God, of being directed by God, of being in the presence of God, of learning to see life through the eyes of God, of being aware of God's love, action, and challenge.

The desert mothers and fathers said that *contemplatio* was best accomplished through manual labor. The ancient literature tells lots of stories about the work that was done by contemplatives— basket weaving, for example, is frequently mentioned.

The link between work and contemplation is very interesting. The desert fathers and mothers were saying contemplation is not idleness. Further, it's not concentration on something else. So who is better for the contemplative life than the person who is working, but not totally caught up in the things he or she is working with? For a person with this approach, work or being busy can become a contemplative act, can be the occasion for fostering the awareness of God's presence.

Many people, I think, sense this. They seem to know intuitively that growing a garden, or painting the house, or raking the leaves are good things to do. Good things happen to people when they are doing such tasks. They use them as a vehicle for bringing their lives to wholeness. That's contemplative. That's coming to awareness. That's giving yourself a chance to see yourself as you are. That's a way of giving yourself a chance to relate your own story to God's story. That's a time you can simply be in the presence of God, and be renewed and revived by that presence. But you have to make time and space for it. Once you make it a practice, it has a way of overflowing even into moments that are consciously being spent reading, working through problems, organizing, administering. Sometimes there are only flashes of awareness, but there is a consistent relationship, a consistent consciousness. I don't think you can deal anyone out of that.

I don't think anyone can live contemplatively without discipline, and that includes your local monk or nun. So, if I am going to live as a contemplative in the suburbs, I am going to have to structure my life, just as a monk or nun must structure his or her life. In both cases, the structure, while it will be different in detail, must be such that it provides regular nourishment for the contemplative dimension of life. This includes regular *lectio*, or spiritual reading, to undergird it and to challenge the way I am living.

People living in the cities and the suburbs, and in our society generally, can make choices about the way they live, though most of them don't see that, because they are conditioned to be on the go all the time, usually at someone else's behest, from early in the morning till late at night.

Imagine for a moment what America would look like, imagine the degree of serenity we'd have, if laypeople had something comparable to the daily schedule of the cloistered life. It provides scheduled time for prayer, work, and recreation.

Of course such a schedule wouldn't look the way mine does as a Benedictine, but it would have the same components—time for work, time for family and community, time for the faith community, time for private scripture reading and reflection. Out of that would come a whole new rhythm of life, a whole new way of seeing the relative importance of various parts of one's life. It could provide the discipline, the structure, to help people make the awareness of the presence of God the greatest value in life.

Some might say this is an unreal expectation in this whirlwind world, but it might be easier than ever before because we have advantages not available in an earlier age. A married woman with children who works outside the home and commutes to work, for example, might not do her *lectio*, spiritual reading, with a book. Instead, she might get the spiritual nourishment provided by *lectio* through listening to a tape while commuting to work or working around the house. This might mean cutting out listening to hard rock or watching *Days of Our Lives*. But becoming a contemplative does involve discipline as well as desire.

And what about her job? Work is not necessarily an impediment to contemplation. We all have to work. St. Benedict knew that. There's a marvelous chapter in the Rule saying, in effect, when you have to get the harvest in, you have to get the harvest in. So pray in the fields! Don't tell me, he's saying, that you left the wheat out in the rain because you had to be home at a certain time to pray, to contemplate. This, the wheat, is what must be attended to now. Do it. This is your contemplation.

When I was a young sister, prayer was my distraction. I couldn't imagine why the prioress couldn't understand there were more important things to do than pray. But after some time of the discipline, prayer became the refreshment, became the thing I couldn't live without.

Contemplation was no longer a burden. It gave meaning to everything else I was doing, no matter how busy I was. It became my center. It gave me direction. It brought me home. I began to see all of my "good works" in relationship to my awareness of the presence of God. This made these "good works" relative. They were no longer my ultimate value. A woman living in the suburbs can do the same with her "good works."

To be sure, you must nourish your awareness of God's presence in your life and in the world. But eventually, it won't be a burden, it won't be an exercise. It *is*. This awareness of God's presence will always be the filter through which you think and act and pray. This presence will always stand between you and over you and around you in everything you are doing.

# Prayer

P rayer is not asking," Mahatma Gandhi wrote. "It is a longing of the soul. . . . It is better in prayer to have a heart without words than words without a heart." In this particular area, though Gandhi's ideas are compelling ones, they are not new ones. The notion of wordless prayer and a hankering soul have been at the very core of monastic prayer life for centuries. As a result, though it is possible to talk about changes in monastic prayer forms, it is not possible to talk about change in monastic prayer life. There are some things which, even as they change, are changeless.

To the monastic mind, prayer is more than a fail-safe mechanism for souls faced with mystery and groveling for forgiveness. It is greater than a sense of spiritual obligation lost in a sea of ceremony. It is beyond a piety awash in fear of a dark and endless universe and in search of favors they cannot assure for themselves. A contemplative tradition regards genuine prayer more as an attitude of the mind in the face of mystery, clinging to hope and steeped in wonder, than simply as a gesture of contrition or obligation or supplication. The differences are not idle distinctions. One type of prayer is not the same as another.

37

What we think to be the purpose of prayer has as much to do with what we pray and the way we pray as the form we adopt in which to do it. In fact, what we think is the purpose of prayer determines the form we adopt. Teresa of Avila, for instance, was targeted as an object of the Inquisition, not because she didn't believe in prayer but because the personal quality of her prayer life—her departure from formula and her level of personal conversation with God—constituted an excursion into the Protestant, according to those charged with guarding the purity of the faith from reformers and recalcitrants alike. God was a potentate to be approached with great protocol, not a personal presence to be cultivated. The form of the prayer was the form of the relationship.

Prayer is neither a passive nor an empty act. On the contrary. Prayer "works." The only problem is that when we pray we get what we seek. What we want out of prayer determines how we go about it. If we want security and protection, we say suffrage prayers; if we want serenity and enlightenment, we meditate; if we want immersion in the mind of Christ, we immerse ourselves in scripture. Prayer is not one kind of activity, it is many. It nourishes the spiritual life; it also reflects it.

When we are young religious, we "say" our prayers. When we get older in the religious life, we "go to prayer." But when we begin to see prayer as the undergirding of life, the pulse of the universe in the center of the soul, we become a prayer. First, as Gandhi says, we have words and no heart; finally, we grow into a heart without words. The truth is that the way we pray says something about what we believe about God and about what we believe about life itself. To the monastic mind, prayer is the marking of time and the pursuit of the known but unseen, the fulfilling but unaccomplished. Those qualities mark the prayer life of a monastic community in both form and substance.

Monasticism, a lifestyle built around the notion of community life and community prayer, changes slowly under any conditions. To bring an entire community to the point of change is not an executive act. It takes months, sometimes years, of preparation to form a community mind around a common concept. Interestingly enough, monastic communities change even more slowly than that where prayer is concerned. The years following the theological renewal of the church which had been inaugurated by Vatican Council II bear testimony to many changes, even in monasteries where time is measured more by the movement of a glacier than the movement of an arrow. But at the same time, some elements of the monastic life have hardly changed at all. Prayer is surely one of them. Consider it a sign of progress. Instead of changing one prayer formula for another, monastics rediscovered the purpose of the first formula and have recovered enough of its meaning and depth to renew them for centuries.

"A childish soul not inoculated with compulsory prayer," Alexander Cockburn wrote in *Corruptions of Empire,* "is a soul open to any religious infection." The thought may bear especially serious reflection in a busy world, even for monastic types. We can get so busy doing so many good things that we don't have time to pray. The soil dries up around our hearts and the tree of life within us dies. Then, a soul crying out for nourishment may be tempted to grasp at any nourishment that goes by, whether it really nourishes the soul or not. With that concern in mind, monastic rules require regularity, ritual, and reflection as hallmarks of monastic prayer life. It is those concepts, not surprisingly, that have become the criteria of change. When those are satisfied, the prayer life of the monastic community is sound, whatever its form and schedule. When those elements are missing, the prayer life of a monastic community goes astray, the community becomes disoriented, meaning fades, and what is meant to be a faith community becomes a collection of strangers doing work they could do with any other group of people in any other place at any other time.

Change has not been foreign to most monastic communities in the last twenty-five years. In fact, one of the signs of a vibrant monasticism has always been adaptation of prayer forms to meet contemporary needs. Benedict's last admonition after twelve chapters of instruction and organization of the daily *ordo* set the tone for the ages: "If anyone sees a better way, let them do it" (RB 18: 22).

Finding a better way to pray is every monastic community's single-minded purpose. It undergirds life. It energizes ministry. It gives substance to the contemplative life. With that in mind, adaptation has been a given; change, however, has not. Monastic prayer, whatever its form, remains forever communal, constantly rhythmic and steeped in ritual. The question is always what must be changed and what must not be changed in order to maintain these qualities at a pitch high enough to bring depth to the daily, one long lifetime after another.

At first glance, the changes common to monastic prayer in the last thirty years seem to be a smorgasbord of popular fads, spiritual styles, or liturgical pop art. In reality, all of them—however inspired by the age and a renewed understanding of the ancient elements of prayer—are more than passing fascination with contemporary style. They represent elements that are essential to monastic spirituality itself but which had been lost over the years under the impact of the prevailing culture or the dictums of the church. Language, silence, brevity, and personal reflection have all been reclaimed from the clutches of formalization, recitation, and overload that characterized the accretions of the ages.

Latin, "the language of the church," distanced monastic communities, along with the church at large, from the richness that lay dormant but only barely visible in the Liturgy of the Hours. With the return of the vernacular to daily prayer, psalms, scripture readings, and literature from the great thinkers of the church, both modern and ancient, became available to communities during prayer time rather than simply as objects of study. With the language of prayer itself no longer a barrier to understanding, prayer became an excursion into thought, into ideas, into statements of faith and moments of insight. Prayer became a period of spiritual development, not merely a time to say the mantras of the faith. Even more interesting, perhaps, is the fact that with the rendering of the Liturgy of the Hours into the language of a particular people, the practice of adding suffrage prayers in English to community prayer periods in Latin—three Hail Marys to St. Florian to protect the community from fire, three Hail Marys to St. Benedict for a happy death—ceased completely. The need to add "devotions" to prayer ended when prayer itself became a devotion.

Language, the use of real language rather than formal language for prayer, restored the Liturgy of the Hours to its place as the spiritual lifeline of the community. Universal language, the elimination of sexist terminology from prayer itself, inserted communities into the center of the human race, called to the community mind the needs and sufferings of all humanity rather than of only half of it, and spoke, at the same time, of a greater God than the inadequate male artifact that had been passing for an all-spiritual Creator for far too long. It made theology true to its best self.

Brevity, too, a by-product of the renewal that shortened some prayer periods and eliminated others, did more than quantity, ironically, to bring depth to community prayer where once profusion of prayers had become more the goal than reflection. With the elimination of the minor Hours, *prime, terce, sext,* and *none*—all designed to have been a Christian response to the Roman changing of the guard in honor of the Emperor-god—morning praise and evening praise, the poles of the day, took their rightful place in the monastic horarium. Resurrection and creation took precedence in a life centered in the paschal mystery.

Community prayer, in the monastic tradition, is designed to inspire personal prayer and reflection, not to smother it with ceaseless recitations. Now there was time to immerse a community in the psalms they were praying, the readings they were hearing, the hymns they were singing. Now there was time to sink into the Liturgy of the Hours itself, to bring the day and all its works to the bar of scripture and to learn from the heart of the psalmody what it is that we are lacking in our own lives.

Personal reflection rather than community recitation became the purpose of prayer. By praying in the language of the culture, eliminating prayer periods that reflected the needs of earlier cultural situations, inserting segments of silence into the prayer periods themselves, communities that prayed became praying communities.

The changes that were adopted did not minimize prayer. On the contrary. The changes restored common prayer to its rightful place in the heart of the community and made it a springboard to the heart of the individual monastic.

In the end, then, little changed at all in the prayer life of monastic communities. Prayer is still said in common, several times a day, in psalmody as old as monasticism itself. But it is said thoughtfully, slowly, with enough room for silence to enable us to listen to the God who is listening to us. Maybe the most important element of prayer that has changed in the last thirty years lies not so much in its forms but in our attitudes toward it. We have stopped "getting prayer in" and started praying again. It is regular, ritualized, and intent on making the monastic reflect on life, its meaning, its purpose, its joys, and its sorrows. Otherwise, prayer is not prayer. It is only a formula, a kind of prayer wheel existence designed to impress God with our fidelity. But the function of prayer is not to coax God to save us from ourselves. The purpose of prayer is to prepare our own hearts for the inbreaking of God, for the putting on of the mind of Christ, for the burst of awareness, when it comes, that God is not somewhere else. God is here, now, in our own hearts. Prayer is simply time put aside to seek the God who has first sought us. Change is not necessary. Unless, of course, it is designed to make changelessness possible. As Gandhi reminds us, "It is better in prayer to have a heart without words than words without a heart."

# Empowerment

*I* approach the topic of empowerment and spirituality with a
great deal of respect and a certain amount of trepidation. After all, we live in a culture that has seen the dark side of both.
Spirituality, clearly, has often been used as an excuse to be hu-
manly irresponsible. And power has too often, God knows, been
made a poor substitute for empowerment.

The fact is that to be real, spirituality must empower, and
power to be holy must be grounded in spirituality. The Talmud
says, "Never pray in a room without windows." Never pray, in other
words, without one eye on the world around you, or your prayer
may become more therapy than energy. And Camus wrote once,
"The saints of our time are those who refuse to be either its executioners or its victims." Spirituality, then, is not for nothing.
Spirituality is not for its own sake. But what is the spirituality of
power and what, exactly, is the power of spirituality? How would
we recognize them if we saw them? How do we know when they
exist and when they do not? And what do they have to say about
the use of authority in the church and the world today?

In the pursuit of these answers, I suggest two companions in the process of coming to understand spirituality and empower-ment: Moses and the Samaritan woman. One, Moses, had enough power to tame; the other, the Samaritan woman, had insight that impelled. The world of our time and the church of our time I believe may well need both.

Moses knew clearly what power was all about. He had over-come the enemy, brought down plagues on the nation, drawn water from a rock, and parted the very sea. Indeed, Moses was an in-spiring figure, a charismatic figure, a powerful figure, who talked to God face-to-face. Moses could well have been a tyrant, an au-thoritarian, a dogmatist, a harsh and exacting lawgiver. But Moses clearly had a spirituality of power that forestalled that. Power was from God, Moses knew, to be used for the things of God. He had contemplated it in the burning bush. He had heard it on the mountaintop. He had felt it at the Sea of Reeds. And he had held it in his own hands with the prophets of Baal.

But the power was not his, and it was not for hoarding. And he knew it. Power, Moses knew, was only given to be given away— and give it away he did. Moses gave his power to the people themselves. Moses, scripture says, chose those who were capable and appointed them as heads over the people. Moses didn't have to be the last word on everything, the final word on the work of God, the only word on the will of God. Moses used his power, too, to plead for their forgiveness from an angry God. "Pardon the iniquity of this people as you have forgiven them ever since Egypt," Moses insisted on behalf of the weary, faithless band whose impunity tested the power of God. And finally, Moses knew that the power he had belonged to God alone. Over the plains at Rephidim while the army of Israel resisted the army of Amalek below, Aaron and Hur held up the tired arms of Moses while he prayed with the staff of God in hand that God would see them through the conflict that he was powerless to change. There was no authoritarianism here, no arrogance here, no domination here.

Indeed, in Moses the spirituality of power is a clear one. Power is not meant to keep a people down; power is meant to build a people up. Power is not meant to be punitive; power is meant to challenge. Power is not meant to be consumed by a few. It is meant to energize the people as a whole. Power is to be wielded, Moses taught Aaron, only by those who judge through the "breastplate of decision," through the eyes of Yahweh, through the very heart of God. The very purpose of power, the only proper use of power, in other words, is empowerment.

The model is surely one we badly need today. In our time, the psychiatrist Rollo May has identified five kinds of power, each of them an exercise for Christian contemplation and a challenge to Christianity itself. May tells us that every act of power is either exploitative, competitive, manipulative, integrative, or nurturing. Exploitation, competition, and manipulation, May teaches, are power used to destroy. Exploitative power is power over another. Competitive power is power used against another. Manipulative power is power used to control another—secretly. We use people and defeat people and control people, in other words, until finally, by destroying them, we destroy ourselves, our worlds, our institutions, our very souls.

Power used to target the globe for extinction is certainly ruthless exploitative power. Power used to suppress the national churches in the name of church unity disunifies while it coerces. Power used against a Hans Kung who questioned with honesty and loyalty his church and who had his permission to teach revoked by the Vatican has got to be a power gone arbitrary. Power used to rape the environment, to poison the water and pollute the air of this globe is power run amok. Power amassed to protect the church from eleven-year-old altar girls and the erotic feet of women and the use of feminine pronouns is power gone inane. Power used to suppress thinkers in a culture and an era more dominated by questions than by answers is a ruthless use of power that will do more in the end to harm us than the questions ever will.

We are living in a world where power is being misused, in a globe that is seething with the issues of women and hunger and poverty and mass migration and nuclear devastation. We are living in a world where both church and state are writing new laws about flags and liturgical dances and language and dress codes while the world is reeling under a massive burden of pain. An ancient proverb states: "To be properly wicked, you do not have to break the law. Just observe it to the letter."

And we wonder why so few are listening anymore. And the deterioration is all around us. These kinds of power are crying for a spirituality that empowers, for a power that pleads, and a power that frees and a power that gentles and a power that cares for the people. Nurturing power and integrative power, May insists, are the only hope of our times. We need a government, we need a people, we need a church whose vast, massive, overwhelming reservoir of power is used to bring people to life and the world together.

The church that spoke out against godless communism in the past must, in the name of God, today use its power to speak out strongly against an unholy capitalism that is devoted to stopping refugees at the borders of the wealthiest nation in the world—our own. We need a government, a people, a church, who use their power to build people up rather than to block them out.

The church that says that man is made in the image and likeness of God must soon, if the very power of God is to be credible in it, begin to see God in the image of woman, too.

The arms race and tokenism and propaganda and patriarchy and the concentration on disloyalty oaths masking as loyalty oaths and the male captivity of the sacraments must give way now to empowerment, to the use of power that works for others and the use of power that works with others. Or wasn't that what the Exodus was for? And wasn't that what Vatican II was all about? Did we misunderstand both the Covenant and the Beatitudes, both Moses's priesthood of the people and the early Christian community, both collegiality and the canonical obligation of the laity—at least according to the new code of canon law—to express our needs and cite our concerns?

And if that's so, what are we saying? Should Luther's questions not have been raised? Should the pope be continuing to free souls only for money? When Innocent III declared England under interdict for having accepted the Magna Carta and limiting the power of a king—a thing, he argued, that was against the natural law—should democracy, therefore, have been forever banned? Has the spirituality of power been reduced to nothing but the trappings of authority? Well, we need prophets now. Let there be no doubt about it. The spirituality of power is key in a modern culture to the existence of the planet, and it is key in the modern church, as well, to the glory of the gospel itself.

To those whose God is system, the criterion for fidelity in times of confusion is seldom only truth. To those who question when the innocent are victimized by an unholy use of power, bureaucrats too seldom preach truth and too often preach obedience. Yet it was a wrong kind of obedience that bred the Inquisition and the cruel crusades. Surely the church deserves a better brand of fidelity than that. And we must remember Moses questioned God.

In times of confusion to those whose God is system, the criterion for fidelity is too seldom an appeal to values held in common and too often an appeal to unity based on silence. But silence was exacted of Galileo, and without gain. In fact, silence was exacted of Galileo with great loss of power to the church. And we must remember Moses argued with God.

In times of confusion, to those whose God is system, the criterion for fidelity is seldom honest search and too often a limiting brand of orthodoxy. But it was the poorest type of orthodoxy that bred the wars of religion.

In times of confusion, those whose God is system say dissent is unacceptable and so make indifference a virtue. Consequently, to save the whole, we so often feed the system martyrs one at a time, whom we then reclaim centuries later and thereby salve our consciences: 100,000 women "witches," Hildegard of Bingen, Erasmus, Meister Eckhart, Pierre Teilhard de Chardin. And yet, it seems, we have no record that the papacy of the Borgia popes was ever officially condemned. Nor do we know of the dismissal of any hierarch anywhere who failed to say a word about the gassing of the Jews, or the selling of slaves, or the extermination of the American Indians.

System is simply no substitute for the gospel. And power is no substitute for empowerment. Where are you, Moses? We need you now.

Nevertheless, a spirituality of power is not enough. We need also those who refuse to be not only executioners but also victims. It is not enough, in other words, to have leaders with a spirituality of empowerment. We need Christians with an empowering spirituality.

Once upon a time a traveler said to one of the disciples, "I have traveled a great distance to listen to the Holy One, but I find the words quite ordinary." And the disciple said, "Don't listen to the words; listen to the message." "And how does one do that?" the traveler asked. "Simple," the disciple said. "Just take hold of the Holy One's sentences and shake them well till all the words drop off. And what is left will set your heart on fire."

Unlike Moses, our second companion on the road to empowerment and spirituality is quite ordinary—as we are, you and I. She is a woman drawing water from a well in Samaria, a small province on the border of Jerusalem. She has obviously struggled through life, making hard decisions, and, as a woman, getting little affirmation from the system. She was full of questions, and full of frustration, but she was full, too, of an uncommon sense of the presence of God and her own obligation to respond to it. The scene is so ordinary, so simple. To really understand it, you have to shake the words off. You have to ask, "What's the real message here? What really happened in Samaria?" Then, finally, you have to ask, as you read the account of the Samaritan woman, "What's really happening to spirituality in the church today?"

In Samaria, it was a revolution going on. The Samaritans, remember, had once been part of the people of God. But they had been conquered by so many empires that they had been cut off for centuries from the country of Judea and from worship in Jerusalem. As a result, they had gradually developed their own interpretation of the books of Moses and their religion had become overlaid with many cultures and with many faiths.

To the Jews, the Samaritans were impostors. They were simply pagans who pretended to be true believers. The hatred between the two groups had hardened over the centuries. No pious Jew would have any contact whatsoever with Samaritans. Jews did not travel into Samaritan territory. Jews did not talk to Samaritans. Jews would not even touch an article that had been handled by a Samaritan—much like white South Africans treated black South Africans not long ago; much like white Americans treated black Americans forty years ago though both called themselves American and both called themselves Christian.

And the even stronger part of the message, of the account of the woman at the well, is the fact that, in those days, too, no good Jew would speak to a woman in public, not to any woman—not to his daughter, not to his mother, not to his wife. The rabbinic law was very clear on that.

And no good Jew even thought about talking theology with a woman. The Rabbi Eliezer had taught quite clearly, "Better that the Torah be burned than placed in the mouth of a woman." No woman had legal credibility. No woman was permitted to give legal testimony in a court of law. What in heaven's name then would a woman know about messiahs and politics and important things? There is no doubt—women and Samaritans were outcasts.

The problem of the church today is that Jesus simply did not share that animosity for either. Jesus was traveling through Samaritan territory. The gospel writer, John, says that Jesus "had to go through Samaria." But that's not true. There was another route then, just as there is now. It simply isn't that Jesus "had" to go. No, the real truth is that Jesus *had* to go. Jesus simply had to go to those people because they, too, were people attuned to life's great search; because God lived, too, in them; because they were listening and because they, too, were spiritual people, people of deep spirituality. And because no one, no one, has a monopoly on the spirit of God.

And there, at that well, in public, Jesus talked to a woman, a Samaritan woman. And Jesus asked for a drink out of a Samaritan bucket. And Jesus even offered to give her water of his own. And then Jesus had a discussion with this woman about some very deep theological things—about the nature of worship, and the nature of salvation and the nature of Jesus, himself. It is to this woman—*it is to this woman*—that Jesus first says in scripture, "I am the Messiah." It is to a woman far outside the boundaries of any system, far outside the spiritual imaginations of orthodoxy, far outside the seats of power, that Jesus gives the word and the promise and the mission. And this Samaritan, this woman, understood who he was. And she went to tell the others. And on her account, the scripture says, they all believed.

The Samaritan woman was an ordinary woman doing ordinary things who got an extraordinary insight into the fullness of life and was given an extraordinary task in a pagan world and they listened to her. She was a prophet, an unacceptable evangelist, a powerless figure, an apostle without portfolio. She wasn't a man—and she was to give the greatest testimony of all time. She wasn't a Jew—and she was to announce the messiah. She was neither politician nor priest, and she was given the gift of understanding and living water and power and empowerment. And they listened to her.

Well, there's a revolution going on in today's church, too. Like the Samaritan woman, people, very ordinary people, are discovering the energy and the insight and the power that comes with the spiritual life. And as it happens when the Holy Spirit gets out of the chanceries of the world, quite ordinary people are being spiritually empowered to seize some gospel decisions of their own. They've come to some spiritual conclusions: that sexism is a sin, that peace is possible, that socialism is not all bad, that capitalism is not all good, that authority has limits and that the Word of God lives, too, in them.

And they're proclaiming those things. And they're demanding those things and they're living those things in the name of the gospel of Jesus Christ. Why? Because Jesus has turned their very ordinary selves, too, and their very ordinary lives into an extraordinary awareness of the presence of God—in them as well as in the powers that be. They have discovered the spirituality that empowers and, like the Samaritan woman, they will not be silenced.

And what the church really needs is more of them to spread the faith instead of the law, to be a sign of hope and contradiction—rather than authority and legalism—in a world that is hungry and ignorant and spending more money and talent and time on the potential destruction of the world and the definition of heresies than on the development of innocent people and the challenge of hard love in a poor, oppressed, groaning, wailing world. With an inner spring welling up inside of them, these spiritually powerful people are the message that God has better plans for us. Because when spiritual empowerment and empowering spirituality explode in people, there is simply no holding back what they have come to see. They know with the philosopher, Ramana Maharshi, "As you are, so is the world."

They know that they have been sent to do the Beatitudes in a world where two-thirds of the people are deprived of the basics of life; they know that they have been sent to be the sign of the call to gospel commitment in a world that wants power and profit instead; they know that they have been sent to become the Christ figure in a world that says, "You get them before they get you," and in a church that says that women are inadequate images of Christ. They know that they have been sent to turn the world around—one heart at a time.

Some people whose power is threatened by the powerless still ask, "What would a woman know, what would a nobody know, about messiahs, about politics, about nuclear war, about values, about church?" And the answer is the same now as then, the same here as at the well. The spiritually empowered know nothing but Jesus. Nothing but the gospel. Nothing but the power within that comes from an empowering spirituality that is not for our own sakes but for the sake of the other. Most of all, they know they have been sent. And they know that somewhere, someday, someone with a spirituality of power will recognize the power of spirituality and listen to them so that the entire world, the whole church, can be empowered. For the sake of the gospel. For the sake of the globe.

And how can we be so sure of all this? Why, simply because we have already seen Moses, the liberator, and the Samaritan woman. We have as model a Moses who was brave enough and faithful enough to trust uncertainty to lead to truth and who used his power to create something new, not to control it. And the Samaritan woman who took power that had not been given to her so that the powerless could have hope.

# Prophecy

⁓

To reflect on a widely known monk from a cloistered community who has been dead more than thirty-five years presumes two questions: First, how was he different? And second, so what?

Thomas Merton's patchwork life is a comfort to the average person. It is at the same time a confusion. Merton was a precocious child, an out-of-control youth, a dissipated young man, a college playboy, an intellectual. Thomas Merton was not the boy next door. He was a man who walked the path from hell to heaven, exposing the journey at every turn so that the rest of us could find hope and meaning in our own journey.

There are several stories that may best explain the influence and the place of Thomas Merton in contemporary society and spiritual development. Two are from the Sufi masters; one is from a personal source.

Once upon a time, the first story tells, some disciples begged their old and ailing master not to die.

"But if I do not go, how will you ever see?" the Master said to them. "But what is it we can possibly see when you are gone?" With a twinkle in his eye, they say, the Master answered, "All I ever did in my entire life was to sit on the riverbank handing out river water. After I'm gone, I trust that you will notice the river."

The lesson rings true. What teachers teach us while they live is one thing; the quality of what they leave us to think about for the rest of our lives is another. Thomas Merton was a fascinating, engaging, offbeat, charming, and provocative personality, true. But what he directed the world to see was far more than the mystique, the mystery of the cloistered life. He left us things worth thinking about for a long, long time.

In the second story, a seeker said to the Master, "Master, I am intent on the spiritual life. May I become your disciple?" And the Master answered, "You are only a disciple because your eyes are closed. The day you open them, you will see that there is nothing you can learn from me or anyone else." "But if that is the case," the seeker said, "what then is a master for?" "The purpose of a master," the Holy One replied, "is to make you see the uselessness of having one."

Thomas Merton's legacy was surely to make us see beyond himself, to bring us to see the rivers around us, to enable us to understand the difference between piety and spirituality, between pseudo and real contemplation, as he did.

The third story is about a fifteen-year-old who read only one "holy" book in the entire sophomore year of high school, and that by accident. The book was called *Seeds of Contemplation,* and the youngster discovered at a much later date that that one book had made everything in life look different.

In fact, Merton leaves all of us with two masterful challenges—to discover the world around us and to find the contemplative spirit within. He did it from a difficult distance, and he did it, at that time, almost alone in a world whose piety was private and whose religion was ritual. He did it in the face of a World War II generation whose sense of life had been jaded by a pervasive presence of violent death, whose idea of development had become unrestrained consumption, whose religion had been sin, sorrow, repentance, and petition for favors from a vending machine and American god, whose notion of freedom was untrammeled individualism, uncritical Americanism, and uncontested international messianism. Merton, the monk, was a leading critic of nuclearism, a voice for nonviolence in a time of civil strife, a pathfinder in East-West interreligious dialogue, a model of globalism, a member of the International Fellowship of Reconciliation, a theologian of ecology, a social analyst, a public figure, a man with an awareness of the feminine dimension of God. On the last day of his life in Bangkok at a conference of Benedictine and Cistercian abbots he told us, "The monastic is essentially someone who takes up a critical attitude toward the world and its structures . . . saying that the claims of the world are fraudulent."

He was, in other words, a genuine contemplative who left insights enough to seed an entire generation in both contemplation and action. Thomas Merton was clearly another kind of monk. Merton was a monastic whose monasticism sprang from a single-minded search for God in life rather than from a single-minded escape from the world for life in God, as ironic as that may seem coming from a cloistered monk.

Merton's monasticism was a revolution equaled only by the origin of Benedictine monasticism itself. Until the 6th century, monasticism had been an exercise in private and personal spirituality. It was Benedict who, in the 6th century, made human community itself the essence of sanctity. Merton's monasticism, too, was a revolution that took monasticism out of the confines of the local monastery and situated it in a concern for world community itself. Merton's monasticism was a monasticism concentrated on the presence of God in the present.

Merton saw the world through a heart uncluttered by formulas and undimmed by systems. He taught more than piety and asceticism for its own sake. He taught concepts that flew in the face of tradition then and fly in the face of culture still: the sin of poverty, the moral imperative of peace, the rectitude of stewardship, the holy power of nonviolence, the sanctity of globalism, and the essence of enlightenment. Merton sowed seeds of contemplation that led to action—an often forgotten but always bedrock spiritual concept.

In Jewish spirituality, for instance, two concepts dominate and are intertwined: The one, *devekut*, translates as "clinging to God" or contemplation; the other, *tikkun o'lam*, translates "repairing the world" or the work of justice. One without the other—contemplation without justice, clinging to mystery without repairing the real world—is unfinished, the tradition teaches, is dark without light, is grand without great, is soul without body.

Scripture is equally clear about the concept as well. Samuel, Solomon, Abraham and David, Judith and Esther, Mary and Mary Magdalene, Matthew, Mark, Luke, John, Peter, and Paul all cling to God, all converse with God. All contemplate the presence of God in life, and all of them are called to do something about it.

Contemplation, Merton teaches us, is learning to see the world as God sees the world. The contemplative sees the world through the eyes of God, and the real contemplative is driven to respond according to the mind of God for it. Clinging to God, in other words, generates the passion it takes to repair the world. Merton's monastic contemplation joins those two concepts again, this time in the face of a culture that is inclined more to rituals than to this kind of contemplative dimension of religion.

Indeed, Merton spent his life dealing out river water to a world yet disinclined to see the river itself but claiming to be following it. Merton handed out river water to soften the dry and sterile ground of religion gone hard, and life gone barren. In *Seeds of Contemplation*, his earliest work, Merton shows us six rivers still running today, still needing our attention: poverty, militarism, ecological stewardship, nonviolence, globalism, and the enlightenment that is contemplation.

*Poverty* and the depths of human indignity it spawns is a river Merton wants us to see. It is in *Seeds of Contemplation* that Merton writes, "Even the desire of contemplation can be impure when we forget that true contemplation means the complete destruction of all selfishness. . . ." It is in *Seeds of Contemplation*, then, that we first come to realize that behind Merton we must come to see the river of poverty that flows outside the pale of a pseudo-contemplation and cloaks itself selfishly in the mysterious and the unreal as a way to avoid God where God really is: in the people who need us.

Consequently, we have a culture seemingly religious that talks soaringly about the lives of its successful but has little or no ear at all for the sagas of those whose lives weave a lesser tale, a culture that sees even religion as the comfort of the self. As a result, some of us find the world a wonderful place to live in. Our newspapers record our progress, our statues remember our public heroes, our cities enshrine our economic temples. But Midtown Manhattan is light years away from Harlem. Trump Tower, where the rich live, is a planet removed from the train tunnels under it where the homeless live. The White House is an entire culture away from the people who have no money, no clout, no power, no highly paid lobbyists to make their case.

The wealthy, Alan Durning writes in *The State of the World*, in the 1990s saw the value of their goods increase 20 times since 1900, the products of their industries 50 times, and their personal travel 1,000 times. Yet, the disparities between the rich and poor of the world have widened obscenely. In the 1990s, this world housed 157 billionaires, and over two million millionaires, but it did not house 100 million homeless at all, while we go to church and we go to church and we go to church. What kind of contemplation is that? What kind of religious action is that?

In this country alone, we spend at least five billion dollars each year to lower our calorie consumption while 400 million people around the world cannot eat at all and so waste away with starved bodies or live with underfed and stunted brains—people we then call "dumb," "stupid," "incapable," "illiterate," "uneducated," "uncouth"—while we hoard grain in barns to use as political power against those for whom death is a happier thought than life. The river of poverty runs through New Delhi and Manila and through New York and Chicago and Miami, as well. Where are the contemplatives who will leave their churches and open their hearts long enough to cling to God by repairing the effects of poverty? Because if we do not, Merton warns us, "Even the desire for contemplation will be impure."

*Militarism* is a river Merton wants us to see. Behind Merton, we must also come to see the river of pain that is caused by the warmongers of the world and which flows alongside the chanting churchgoers who see God outside the world instead of within it. Merton insisted in *Seeds of Contemplation*, "People who know nothing of God and whose lives are centered on themselves imagine that they can only 'find themselves' by asserting their own desires and ambitions and appetites in a struggle with the rest of the world. . . ." And our age, perhaps, has done it best, and done it globally while we protest that we are a nation under God.

Both the bishop of Boston and the bishop of Baghdad, for instance, called the first war in the Persian Gulf "just." Surely there is something wrong either with the theory or with the theology of those who call themselves religious if the theory of the just war can be read totally differently and with the same ease by all sides at the same time.

In our time, too, for the first time in history, we have justified the extermination of women and children on the grounds that indiscriminate assaults against civilians saves soldiers. It is time, surely, to contemplate the possibility that what we really need to contemplate now, in our time, is a theory of the "unjust war."

And what we have not destroyed with weaponry itself—a modern blitzkrieg called "shock and awe"—we have destroyed simply by the making of those weapons. We have used our best minds, our best resources, and the bulk of our national budget to build what will destroy people rather than to build what will develop them. "Our policy," the president says, is to "leave no child behind." But if we go on skewing the national budget for the sake of a new kind of military imperialism, we will, in the end, have left every child behind. We have seduced our industries, our university system, and even the religious community into equating security with militarism. And we have paid a great price for it. To satisfy our vampire's appetite for militarism, we have threatened the level of human services available in this country: schools, hospitals, housing, welfare, the arts. We have absorbed the resources of other nations that it takes to make or base our weapons and so dimmed the hopes of the children of the future.

According to over thirty research organizations in the United States, during that six-week war we fought so gloriously in the Gulf in 1991, here at home 1,240 children died from the effects of poverty; 4,000 infants died due to low birth weight; 68,750 young people dropped out of school; and 4,000 workers became unemployed—all conditions we say we now can't afford to fix. Clearly, war kills everyone, even those who are lucky enough to win it.

In Vietnam, they inflated the number of casualties and conquests to effect victory. In the first Gulf War they at least showed us corpses in burned-out jeeps in the searing desert. Ten years later, in Afghanistan, they showed us nothing at all—except the hole in the middle of our own New York. There were no refugee camps, no estimate of the number of Afghan civilians whose lives had also been ended, one way or another, by the collapse of their country and its nonstop pummeling. Oh, every once in a while a picture seeped through the net: an Afghan baby eating a mudpie made of grass "and a trace of wheat flower" because of the food shortage, a child whose leg had been amputated by a land mine, a village in rubble.

After days, months, of nonstop bombing, both in Afghanistan and in Iraq, we were apparently, somehow, waging a war without victims. At great cost. With no public discussion of its internal implications for either country—and countries around the globe—other than the fact that we were hit and so we hit "them" back. Worse, anyone who tried to discuss other dimensions of the situation was called "unpatriotic." Writers lost their jobs. Peace groups who pleaded for less barbaric means of conflict resolution in a world dangerous to itself were ridiculed. A terrible silence reigned. A fearful silence reigned.

The fact may be that we lose as much as we win in war. We lose our humanity, perhaps, because we have failed to contemplate that the river of pain that runs through the world cannot be staunched by force and the failure of reason.

*Ecological stewardship* is a river Merton wants us to see.

Behind Merton, because of Merton, we must come to see the river of human debris that gushes past the pious "contemplatives" who substitute praying for a prayerful respect for the cycle of nature and the circle of life. "A tree gives glory to God first of all by being a tree," Merton taught us in *Seeds of Contemplation*. "This particular tree will give glory to God," Merton went on, "by spreading out its roots in the earth and raising its branches into the air and the light in a way that no other tree before or after it ever did or ever will do." "The special clumsy beauty of this particular colt . . . this particular April sky . . . that great, gashed, half-naked mountain are all holy in the sight of God, all imitate God," Merton wrote.

But one at a time, we are destroying them, unconsciously, carelessly, callously. We are missing the river. But we call ourselves religious, disciples, a chosen people "under God." "Life is the greatest bargain," the Yiddish proverb says, "we get it for nothing." But we have come to treat it as nothing, too. We have spoiled our nests as no animal would do and we justify it in the name of "maintaining a standard of living" that is making the globe unlivable and being human inhumane.

Air pollution was cited by scientists as a serious problem in the early 1970s. The data was clear then. A political commitment to curb industrial waste that would soften campaign coffers or lose votes or yield international economic supremacy, however, definitely was not.

According to scientist Hilary French in a 1990 World Watch report, severe health problems related to air pollution now cover the globe. In the United States, French says, 150 million people, almost half the population of the country, breathe air considered unhealthy by the Environmental Protection Agency. In Hungary, every seventeenth death is caused by air pollution. In India, French confirms, breathing the air in Bombay is equivalent to smoking ten cigarettes a day. And in Mexico, the capital city with notoriously noxious air is considered, irony of ironies, a hardship post for diplomats of countries who go to conferences on the environment but refuse to agree to pollution standards that would clear it up. The environmental impacts are even more startling: acid rain and air pollution are decimating crops and devastating forests and destroying lakes and buildings, too, even in the industrialized countries of the world. "Till the garden and keep it," the scripture mandate, has become "seize the garden and rape it." And we have yet to elevate the survival of the globe to the level of a moral concern.

*Nonviolence* is a river Merton wants us to see. Behind Merton, because of Merton's call to contemplation, we must come to see as well the river of nonviolence. Real contemplatives know all creation to be a piece of God's presence in the world and so to be reverenced and treated tenderly. Violence has simply run its course: War is now obsolete. War is much more than conflict; it is social annihilation. Human relations on such a grand scale require cooperation, not coercion.

What we destroy we defeat, true, but most of all we destroy something in ourselves. What we do to one another gouges out the center of our own lives. To napalm children is to pour acid on our own souls.

To bomb an innocent people, an illiterate people, a destitute people into tent cities on foreign borders as we did in Afghanistan, babies in their bellies and old people on their backs, is obscene. To reject the cry to deliver food to people living on vegetation while we eat carrot cake, while we boast that we are not targeting civilians, is to shift the moral question away from terrorism to the integrity of bombing.

To turn whole city neighborhoods and towns to ash overnight as we did in Iraq, to throw an entire country into economic disarray, bomb out their electrical grids and water supplies, stand by while their most ancient treasures of world significance are looted, and—according to a report prepared by an affiliate of the organization International Physicians for the Prevention of Nuclear War—to kill over 22,000 civilians while claiming that we do not make war on the innocent is a most sophisticated lie.

To duplicate in them what has happened to us, in order to show their governments—the very people we put in place, the very people whose control we engineered—that we will not tolerate their resistance to our plans and policies, is not to bring justice to the world. It is simply to continue the cycle of vengeance on the innocent which will live on against us in their children while the violent still go free. Or as the Roman philosopher Seneca said of it: "They make a desert and call it peace."

War has become the pitting of one group of invisible combatants against another group of defenseless noncombatants and cannot therefore possibly be called "just" by any theological measure, here or anywhere else.

To refuse restraint, to subordinate focused search and capture missions, stronger financial strategies, heightened international intelligence work, increased domestic security to carpet bombing, cluster bombs, and cruise missiles raises serious moral questions about the effect of localized force on tiny cells of international terrorists somewhere else.

To refuse nonviolent means of conflict resolution, to set up commissions and committees of war chiefs and warlords, military advisors and consultants, and not to have so much as one member of the peace academy, not one expert in nonviolent conflict resolution, not one refugee, not one representative of the real victims at the table, is certain to determine the outcome without asking the question.

To refuse to sign protocols that would set up a world court and then wonder why there is no world coalition when justice is needed most; to take away civil rights of privacy, law, and citizenship in the name of protecting civil rights; to practice totalitarianism in the name of democracy is to mock what we say we stand for. It is to destroy by our own hands what we say we are securing.

And then to wonder why guns become the playthings of children, or why families are torn apart by domestic murders, or why women are routinely beaten, or why drugs become the desensitizer of choice in a world where violence is social and economic and domestic policy as well as military, is to raise denial to the level of high art. Indeed, the blood of our own children runs red in our streets because we have taught our children violence very well—and they have learned it quickly. We are reaping what we have sown. We are getting what we asked for.

How can we possibly convince them that their violence is bad but our violence is good if we keep justifying the decimation of peoples in the name of God?

Into that climate of nationalism and chauvinism and unholy righteousness came Thomas Merton in *Seeds of Contemplation* with waters of loving nonviolence. "To say that I am made in the image of God," Merton says, "is to say that love is the reason for my existence, for God is love." "Because God's love is in me," he wrote to us, "it can come to you from a different and special direction that would be closed if God did not live in me . . . and because it is in both of us, God has greater glory. God's love is expressed in two more ways in which it might not otherwise be expressed."

"Violence in a house," the rabbis say, "is like a worm in fruit." It destroys what otherwise looks healthy and firm and good but which is harboring within it the cause of its own decline. Violence is eating the heart right out of this country—in private homes and police stations, in personal relationships, playgrounds and public policies. Violence is our national disease. Walking gently through life is our only real hope of gentling the world. God's love, Merton teaches us, can only come through me. The love of God for which I seek can only come through you.

*Globalism* is a river Merton wants us to see. Behind Merton, we must come to see as well the river of globalism that flows through the real contemplatives who find God everywhere.

"The more I become identified with God," wrote Merton in *Seeds of Contemplation*, "the more I will be identified with all the others who are identified with God." "We are members one of another," he wrote in an intellectually insular USA, "and everything that is given to one member is given to the whole body."

"The saints are glad to be saints," he told us in a new and powerful insight into sanctity, "not because their sanctity makes them admirable to others but because the gift of sainthood makes it possible for them to admire everybody else . . . , it delivers them from the burden of judging others and condemning them." And he told us that in a world that suspected almost everybody and saw the world as a place to be evangelized into Western culture, U.S. politics, white power, and uncurbed capitalism.

He saw the world as good, its many peoples as gifts of the

same God, its religions as many manifestations of the one God, its differences a revelation to the world. He asked us to open our eyes and see what no law ever taught: that life is not a set of boundaries; life is a river of possibilities to be cultivated, a tide of differences to be respected, to be held in awe.

When people are doing our work for wages we ourselves would not accept, we must begin to ask what there is about us that enables us to exploit them. When U.S. industries engage in business practices on the international level that would not be allowed in our own country we must begin to ask, if we are really contemplatives, what is it in our own souls that allows us to treat other people as if they were not people at all. When the resources of the world are controlled by the few, when the mineral deposits of one nation are held hostage by another, we must begin to ask, if we are really contemplatives, whether there isn't already an international welfare system where the poor nations support the rich ones, and haven't we created it while we deny our own poor the same.

Where are the contemplatives like Merton who will begin to see, who will begin to ask at what moral peril we have bought our wealth and our power and our standard of living? "It is God's love that speaks to me in the birds and streams," Merton said in *Seeds of Contemplation*, ". . . but if God's will would grow from my freedom, I would become the love that God is. . . ." When the starving sick lie dying on subway grates, if I am a contemplative, Merton would say, I must become the love that God is.

When the underemployed workers in Detroit lose their homes and their dignity, I must become the love that God is. When the blacks die in Soweto because they are black, and kill one another in the housing projects of Chicago because they are in despair at being black in a white world, I must become the love that God is. When Iraqi children die in American wars, and crack babies languish on our own streets, if I am really a contemplative, I must become the love that God is.

Globalism, to Merton, is the ability to open my heart and my mind, my arms and my policies to the whole world, not simply the world that is my color, my class. No mastery of past pious disci-

plines—no matter how time-honored, no matter how good—substitutes, in Merton's mind, for real contemplation, for the ability
to see with the eyes of God.

*Enlightenment,* real contemplation, is a river Merton wants us
religious types to see. Merton calls us all to another way of looking at life and another way of living it. Merton calls us, leads us,
to the river of enlightenment. "Go into the desert," Merton teaches
us in *Seeds of Contemplation,* "not to escape others but in order to
find them in God." No amount of religious ritual, no quantity of
religious reading, no degrees in religious history will forgive us
the responsibility to be religious people, to bind the world together again in God.

Once upon a time, the Sufi tell, a master whose disciples were
about to go on the salvific pilgrimage gave them each a bitter
gourd to take with them into every holy shrine for every holy
prayer. When the disciples returned from their holy and sanctifying journey, the master requested that each of the acrid gourds be
cooked for the welcome home dinner. "Ah," the master said, as the
disciples gagged on the biting taste, "I see that no amount of holy
water has been able to sweeten what was sour."

Over and over again, Merton tells us in *Seeds of Contemplation*
that simply living the law and repeating the ritual is not enough.
Merton calls us to sweeten what is tinged with sharp in us, to
repair what is broken in us, to cling to the God who is God, yes,
but for the sake of a whole hurting world gone sour, not simply
for my own spiritual satisfaction.

The person with the enlightened heart knows that the purpose of the human voice is to give sound to the voiceless until, finally,
the world begins to hear what the enlightened heart has come to
know—God's presence here, now, in everyone. Where the person
stands who has an enlightened heart is more like the reign of
God than it was before they got there: the property is beautiful,
the litter is gone, the street is safe, the stranger is welcomed,
the poor are fed, the refugee is housed, the works of war become
works of peace. Nothing else is acceptable to Merton. Nothing
else is called holy because any other defilement of life says that

the world belongs to me rather than that I and it belong to God.

The person with an enlightened heart is on earth to care for it, not to consume it. The person with an enlightened heart is detached from what holds the world in the grip of money lust and patriarchal power. Once upon a time, the Sufi say, a Holy One said to the businessman, "As the fish perished on dry land, so you perish when you get entangled in the world. The fish must return to the water; you must return to God." The businessman was aghast. "Are you saying that I must give up my business and go into a monastery?" And the Holy One said, "No, no, hold on to your business and go into your heart." Merton's concept of contemplation leads to the same insight: There are two things that corrode the human endeavor: wanting more of everything and never knowing the meaning of enough.

The person with an enlightened heart is emptied of the need to take up all the space and use up all the goods and grind up all the people. No ethnic jokes are ever told by the person with an enlightened heart; no sexist language is ever used; no racial slurs are ever uttered. No enemy bashing is ever practiced. People are people, not colors or sexes or ages or types.

Enlightenment is the ability to see beyond all the things we make God, and find God. We make religion God and so fail to see godliness where religion is other, though goodness is clear and constant in the most different of people, in the remotest of places.

We make national honor God while refugees pour by the thousands through all the porous borders of the world, and of every hundred people alive only thirty are white. Which, incidentally, makes whiteness as a norm of anything quite suspect.

We fail to see the presence of God in other nations, particularly non-Christian nations. We make personal security God and fail to see God in others' needs on those bleak and barren days when life seems fragile and our own future unsure.

We make human color and gender the color and gender of God and fail to see God in the one who comes in different shades and other forms, though our scriptures are clear about equality and our theology is sound.

We separate spirit and matter as if they were two different things, though we know now, from quantum physics, that matter is simply fields of force made dense by the spirit of energy that is the base of everything. We are one with the universe, in other words. We are not separate from it or different from it.

And we are not above it. And we are in it—all of us and everything—swimming in an energy that is God. And so we are not separate from one another, or different from each other either. We are, each of us, simply one more sliver of humanity seeking to become more human, trying to be godly, and we will never be it either by diminishing ourselves or by degrading others.

To be enlightened is to see behind all the forms life takes to the God who holds them in being. Enlightenment sees, too, behind the shapes, icons, and language that intend to personalize God to the God who is too personal, too encompassing, to be any single shape or form or name.

Enlightenment takes us beyond our parochialisms to the presence of God everywhere, in everyone, in the universe. It ignores color. It disdains gender. It releases gifts and listens to voices not its own precisely because they are not its own.

To be enlightened is to be in touch with the God within us and around us, in ourselves and in others, more than it is to be engulfed in any single way, any one manifestation, any specific denominational or nationalistic or sexual construct, however good, however well-intentioned that kind of benign ungodliness may be.

God is radiant light, blazing fire, asexual spirit, colorless wind. God is the magnet of our souls, the breath of our hearts, the stuff of our lives. God is no one's pigment, no one's flag, and no one's gender. And those who certify their God under any of those credentials make a new idol in the desert. To be enlightened we must let God speak to us through everything—and everyone—through whom God shines in life.

It is a practice in many monasteries of my order as we process into chapel for prayer to bow first to the altar, yes, but then to turn and bow to the sister who is walking in procession with us.

The meaning of such a monastic custom, a gesture common to monasticisms around the world, in fact, is clear: God is as much in the world around us, as much in one another, as on that altar or in that chapel. The great ecumenical mind, the great contemplative spirit, the great peacemaking heart magnifies the meaning of that gesture to the level of the universal. It makes visible, demonstrable, present, and overpowering the goals for which all religions—Buddhist, Hindu, Jewish, Christian, Muslim—exist.

"The ultimate perfection of the contemplative life," Merton insists, in *Seeds of Contemplation*, "is not a heaven of separate individuals, each one viewing a private vision of God; it is a sea of love. . . . God is the life of all of us and we are all one in God." We are all one with Nelson Mandela, and we are all one with Yasser Arafat, and we are all one with Saddam Hussein, and we are all one with the children in the squatter's settlements of South Africa, and we are all one with the AIDS patients in the San Francisco hospices, and we are all one with the people in Afghanistan whose homes we destroyed and have yet to restore as we promised. We are all one, the contemplative knows, so it is not just that their salvation depends on us. The fact is that our salvation depends on how we deal with Timothy McVeigh and Saddam Hussein and child murderers whom we have trained to kill. The person with an enlightened heart sees hospitality as the tabernacle of the world. Either God is in the other or God is not, and if God is in the other we dare not leave them out.

There are some things that the contemplative, the person with an enlightened heart, simply will not do because they contribute to the destruction of the world rather than to its development. The person with an enlightened heart, for instance, will not promote weaponry. The person with a monastic heart will not buy a T-shirt or a toy or a bumper sticker or a banner that glorifies war. The person with an enlightened heart will not poison the land or foul the waters or dump waste in foreign countries so that the poor there will die from what makes the wealthy here richer. The person with an enlightened heart advocates for policies that work for the poor and the homeless and the underemployed as well as the secure. The person with an enlightened heart remembers the forgotten generation of children who need day care and lunch and the arts and opportunities of life if the next generation is to have the possibilities and the quality that marked the last. The person with the enlightened heart realizes that the questions of this age cannot be answered with the limited vision of the past.

The person with Merton's enlightened contemplative heart knows that war has gone far beyond the conflict of armies to the ruination of whole civilizations; knows that poverty is not an accident of nature, it is the foreign policy of wealthy nations and the debt crisis of ones made poor due to the ravishing by other ones; knows that the globe is not a cosmic garbage dump; knows that force only triggers force and makes things worse, and that the only thing we have yet to try on violence is nonviolence.

The person with Merton's enlightened contemplative heart knows that the globe has no natural boundaries, only unnatural divisions. Indeed, Thomas Merton has sat on the riverbank doling out water for over fifty years. He sowed seeds of contemplation that changed the mentality of the world and sowed the seeds of soul that let loose the force of radical action. Like those Benedictine monastics before him who brought order to a ruined empire and gave agriculture back to a stampeded civilization and reforested the stony valleys of Europe, and saved the learning of the ages by copying the books themselves, Merton hearkens us back to the values that saved civilizations before us so that a civilization desperately in need of peace and nonviolence and stewardship and a sense of the divine in the mundane can be saved again—if we will only see the rivers to which his life points.

It is not an easy task but it has succeeded, if not for all, at least for many; if not for many, at least for me. I do not know who the first master was who was a giver of water. I do not know who the first master was to tell us that there was a religion so religious that it far exceeded the law. But one thing I do know for sure. I know that Merton seeded young hearts as well as old because I was the fifteen-year-old who read *Seeds of Contemplation* fifty years ago and was never the same again.

I learned from Merton, for instance, that the rivers of poverty and war and planetary poison rage around us while we claim religiosity. I also learned that the rivers of peace and nonviolence and globalism are possible if we will only contemplate God long enough, practice *devekut* and *tikkun o'lam* deeply enough, come to see God clearly enough, want God intensely enough to find God where God really is: here, all around us, within us, and within the ones born in stables and driven from the temples of the world, as well. Indeed, contemplation is not an easy task. It cannot be done in isolation. It cannot be done for its own sake.

The Sufi tell the story of the Holy One who was walking along the flooding banks of a raging river when suddenly he saw a scorpion clinging to a tree branch only inches above the swollen stream. "Poor thing," the Holy One said. "Scorpions can't swim. If the waters reach that hanging branch, it will surely drown."

And then the Holy One dropped to the ground and began to crawl along the branch toward the scorpion. But every time the Holy One touched it, it stung the hand that reached to rescue it. A passerby said firmly, "Don't you realize that if you try to handle that scorpion, it will sting you?" "Of course," the Holy One said, "but simply because it is the scorpion's nature to sting does not mean that I should abandon my human nature to save."

Merton shows us a contemplation steeped in action, a clinging to God that demands the repair of the world, an enlightenment that leads to change and hope and holiness. My prayer for people who steep themselves in Merton is that they also steep themselves in a God who is in the world calling us all to a new enlightenment of heart, beyond the law, beyond the books, to a long look at God where God is and where God is not, to the contemplation that leads to action. The ages are full proof: sting it must, this contemplation of God in reality, but for the sake of those who live in hope of a better world, save it will. Sting it must, but save it surely will if we finally come to realize that though nothing we do changes the past, everything we do changes the future.

# Wholeness

*J*onathan Edwards once wrote: "Saints do not see things others
do not see. On the contrary. They see just what everyone else
sees—but they see it differently." The question is, what do we see
in our time, and how do we see it? And what does that have to do
with being a woman and a person of faith? Or to put it another
way, what does that have to do with being a person of faith, whether
you are a woman or not?

The situation which we are required to see is a vast, complicated, crucial, and obviously skewed one: two-thirds of the hungry of the world are women; two-thirds of the illiterate of the
world are women; two-thirds of the poor of the world are women.
The ozone layer—the placenta of the earth—has been rup-
tured. The polar ice caps are melting and raising the water levels
of the world, while at the same time the lands of the poor are
turning to dust and stone.

Chemicals which once activated the soil are now depleting it,
and fertilizers used to energize our land are now polluting our
rivers and lakes.

Water, air, trees, and land are destroyed everywhere: fertile fields, rain forests, tropical gardens, oceans, lakes and rivers, have been raped, ravaged, spoiled, soiled, and poisoned.

Two hundred million animals a year are wantonly destroyed— for "research"; species after species becomes extinct.

Nuclear weaponry threatens the very existence of the planet and has the effrontery to call itself "defense," and all the while a world filled with churchgoers is also filled with the obscenely poor. Clearly, we have not reached the point of seeing "differently." It is possible that we have not reached the point of seeing at all.

The questions are, then: what relationship, if any, is there between theology, ecology, and feminism? What underlies the conflict between them? And what, on the other hand, urges—even demands—their conjunction?

In 1960, Lynn White Jr. wrote an essay that shook the theological givens of the period, but is now recognized as a classic statement of theological concern. The major problem facing the modern world, White argued in "The Historical Roots of Our Ecological Crisis," is that the Judeo-Christian ethic justifies domination. What people do and fail to do about ecology-of-life issues depends, White posited, on what people think about creation, think about themselves, and think about their relationship to things around them.

If water has no value of its own except for my use, then I can dam it up, drain it off, drown it in oil and waste and tin cans until it chokes the fish and poisons the children.

What our Western religious tradition teaches us to think, White said, is hierarchy, superiority, and domination. The question is why? And the answer I believe is because we have chosen to emphasize one creation story over the other, and used the second one to prove it, and as a result, we have lost our balance and forgotten our way.

We cannot deny that Christianity is the most anthropomorphic of all religions. It begins by centering on the creation of humanity. It proceeds by glorifying it. And it ends concerned solely with the redemption of humanity.

The progression of those concepts is clear. First, Christianity teaches, Creation is a procession of stages, each plane higher than the last. From this viewpoint, humanity outranks the universe in splendor and achievement. It is, therefore, moral, Godly, to put our needs above the needs of other creatures.

Second, Man—the male—is the crown of creation. Men said so. Therefore, what women think or want or need is, at best, secondary, without priority. And what men say that women think or want or need becomes "a woman's place," "the law of the land," the "will of God" for them. Or to put it another way, everything written about us is written without us.

Third, God planned the world for human benefit, we insist. "You," the story teaches, "can have everything in the garden." Creation, the traditional redaction implies clearly, is a cornucopia of creature comforts designed to satisfy the unlimited desires of humankind while pollution circles the earth in eleven days and whole forests disappear daily.

Fourth, "Man," like God, we argue, transcends nature, and has it for his use and all for nothing, no cost incurred.

Therefore, fifth, the function of physical creation is to serve man's purpose, whatever its scope.

We assume with confidence, sixth, that we are above nature—are not nature! Despite the fact that as the top of the food chain we will be the first to go if pollution continues at the present rate.

Because we are made "in God's image," we conclude, we are also God's agents on earth. Free. Autonomous. Unrestrained.

"Fill the earth and subdue it, rule over every living creature," we repeat to ourselves. Again. And again. And again. No caveat given; no caution entertained; no balance struck.

And the lesson has been well-learned.

Those who have the resources to dominate, dominate the resources. Those who lack the power to dominate become a resource. No morals lost; no ethic spoiled; no sin sinned.

The conclusions and applications of that kind of thinking are painfully, dangerously, clear: gone are the sacred groves. Nature has no reason for existence except to serve human existence. Time is linear and a process of perpetual progress. Time becomes eternity, and the eternal is meant simply for the endless replenishment of time.

In a world such as this, a sense of "enoughness" is a sign of mental aberration. A desire for "moreness" is a sign of human progress.

Humans are superior to nature, but men—males—the real crown, the pinnacle, the divine pride of creation, are superior to women. Or, to be more direct, women are other than men, and therefore lower than men. "A helpmate fit for man" we translate Genesis to say. According to David Friedman, "ezer kenegdo" normally translated as "power equal" everywhere in scripture but here. And "helpmate" —not leader, not thinker, not visionary has woman, therefore, been allowed to be.

In the hierarchy of creation, women, obviously, as philosophy taught and the churches theologized, were suited for things of the body—things of nature, natural things. Men, on the other hand, whose bodies were not suited for anything inherently creative, must then, men reasoned, be clearly suited for the things of the soul—the things of the mind, of course—the spiritual things of life, obviously. Man/the male was closest to God, the theologians argued, because it is the mind that reflects the essential attribute of God—the spirit.

In the hierarchy of creation, then, instead of gaining because they have both creative body and rational soul women are defined by their bodies and robbed of the quality of their souls. So spoke Augustine, Origen, Thomas Aquinas. "Not in the body but in the mind," Augustine wrote, "was man made in the image of God"; and woman, they argued, was "derived"—was made in the image of man—rather than as scripture says clearly, formed from the same material, bone-bone, flesh-flesh. So spoke them all. So speak them still.

The thought process is plain: God, spirit, is the ultimate. And so matter, nature, is without value. Nature loses—and woman loses, too. With that theology, the foundation is laid for a science that came out of that theology, to assert the subjugation of nature that follows from it. The destiny of the human race and the fate of the planet with it, was sealed by a science, rationalized by a theology and predicated on a divine domination embodied in human agency.

When Francis Bacon in the seventeenth century introduced the experimental method to science—the gathering of data to gain power over nature—he based his justification for the process on the unarguable—on theology. There was no doubt about his premise: "Man fell," Bacon said, "and lost dominion. But he can regain it through scientific study." The new high priests of the time became its scientists. "Nature," Bacon said, "is to be bound into service—like a slave." The premises of a science based on a theology of domination led to the obvious. Since there was no spirit in nature, there was nothing in nature to respect. After that, we're in scientific free fall.

Descartes enthroned dualism, and named matter subservient. Newton said matter was only instrument, and the mechanists regarded matter as simply an inert stage for human activity.

The coup was now complete: Nature was lifeless, manipulable, valueless, eternally subordinate. Clearly, science and theology were not natural enemies. On the contrary—science and theology made for the perfect marriage. The theologians rested everything on the superiority of spirit. The scientists concentrated on the subjugation of matter. Then, everything falls into place: Darwin introduced the idea of the survival of the fittest. And the social Darwinism of the Industrial Revolution, colonialism, and "development" based on science became its necessary and dangerous corollaries.

Clearly it was true: we could do whatever we wanted with any "other" less human than we—indigenous/aborigines/blacks/women/gays/lesbians. We could take what we wanted from everywhere. We could squeeze the earth dry of what we wanted anywhere and make the rest of the world sinfully poor because it had all been made for humans. For us. For the fittest and, therefore, for the fittest of us. And the "fittest" of us were clearly not women.

Now theology, ecology, and sexism were of a piece: After all, religion said that the "order of creation" was determinate, biblically inviolable. Man was created first, before woman, the theologians argued, and was therefore superior—no mention of the apes that preceded him, of course, or how it got to be, in that case, that woman, created last, was not clearly God's perfect achievement.

Hierarchy was a given. Men were on top of the pyramid and women were the bottom of the bottom.

And science confirmed what theology taught: that women were "natural" by virtue of a physiology designed for birthing rather than thinking. Woman becomes a symbol of what every culture uses, needs, depends on, and devalues—nature itself. Mothering was defined as a lifelong process, fathering an isolated, a momentary event. Therefore women—naturally—"belong" in the home. Men—naturally—are the proprietors of religion and politics, of culture and thought. Women are "particularistic," given to the minor details of life, the philosopher Claude Levi-Strauss theorized. Men, on the other hand, physically free of natural tasks, are universalistic—men surmount the particular. They transcend the mundane.

Woman is symbol-using, yes, but inferior, intermediate, instrumental, a glorified potted plant. And they said so, philosophers and theologians alike, over and over again.

Rousseau said a woman could be educated, but only for the advancement of her husband. Mill said a woman could be educated, but only in order to be fit to maintain the social standards set by men. In 1969, Levi-Strauss said a woman could be educated in order to maintain the domestic system on which men depend to control the public one. And in the 1990s Pope John Paul II said that women had "a special nature" for "a special purpose." To maintain the home, but not the theology, the ministry of the sacraments of the church.

The patriarchal worldview that follows from those premises is a clear one: it is hierarchical in structure, dominative in essence, dualistic in evaluations, and male in its norms. Clearly, what underlies the conflict in theology, ecology, and feminism is the theology of domination; the notion that some of us were made to be—meant to be—better than the rest of us, that some of us are in charge of the human race and we know who we are. That is the theology of domination.

But the theology of domination is a recipe for conflict, struggle, suppression, oppression, and revolution. And we are in it. And it is everywhere. We can surely see that, at least.

There can be no doubt about it: we need a new worldview. And we need it now. Why? Because the world is shifting.

If the earth's population were a village of 100 people, there would be 62 Asians, 12 Europeans, 8 Africans and only 13 "villagers" from the Americas. Seventy of them would be non-white. Sixty-seven would be non-Christian. Fourteen could not read. Twenty-one would be undernourished. One of them would have a college education and two of them would own a computer. And fifty-nine percent of the entire wealth of that village would be held by only six people, and all of them would be white, male, from the United States of America. No wonder those six buy so many guns. The world is tilting and tipping and is terribly out of kilter.

But how shall we build this new worldview? Where can it come from? In fact, what is it and how is it happening? If they want to be building blocks of the new worldview, science and ecology, theology, and feminism will have to be reconciled.

First, Christianity must remember that God pronounces all of creation "good," not just some of it good, some better, some best.

Second, Christianity must realize that human responsibility for the earth requires care, not sovereignty.

Third, Christianity must revive its sense of sacramentality, that all things reveal the creative presence of God.

Fourth, Christianity must honor human finiteness, that humans are simply part of creation—its most contingent, its most vulnerable, its most fragile part, indeed. All the rest of creation, in fact, can live without humanity. It is only humanity that is totally dependent on the rest of creation for its existence.

Fifth, Christianity must come to see that it is the Sabbath, the contemplative mind that is the crown of creation, not "man."

Finally, sixth, Christianity must rediscover Genesis 2, the companionship story, and begin to see it differently.

The truth is that in Genesis 2 God brings all the animals to Adam to be named. To be known, in other words. To be brought into relationship with.

No one looks into the eye of an animal, names it, and then kills it. We name domestic animals—the ones we take into the family; the ones we take responsibility for; the ones we relate to on an individual basis. Surely Genesis 2, the companionship story, puts Genesis 1, the stewardship story, in perspective. The scripture is astoundingly clear: by bringing the animals to the human for naming, God demonstrates that it is relationship, not domination, not individualism, that makes humankind "like God."

Individualism is theologically bankrupt. The "common good" includes all of creation, including the non-human. But if that is the case, males are hardly autonomous and certainly not the universal norm of anything.

Sexism, therefore, is heresy, is pathological pride, is hubris raised to high art. The truth is that science has rediscovered theology for us—and calls it ecology. Science knows now that everything is interrelated; that humanity is only one aspect of the fabric of life; that our connectedness is infinitely complex, and that, having poisoned the earth and polluted the air, we are now on the verge of extreme natural degradation and irreversible natural changes. If we do not see our sin and call it that, the anthropocentric—human-centered—worldview has failed us, has left us spiritual orphans. The androcentric—male-centered—worldview has destroyed us, has left us spiritual amnesiacs, has put us in contention with ourselves, with the universe, and with God the creator.

The world does not exist for us alone. On the contrary. Diversity is necessary. It is diversity we degrade and it is diversity we destroy. But it is specialization that is entropic. It is specialization that kills. If we farm only one product, the land dies; if we insist on only one social system, creativity dies; if we honor only one culture, peoples die; if we elevate only one sex, the fullness of humanity dies.

That is why feminism confronts androcentrism, this simplification of life to a one-gendered viewpoint only. Because simplification isn't good for anyone. It's not good for women. It's not good for the planet. It's not even good for men—it isolates them emotionally, it distorts them socially, it overdrives them physically and makes impossible demands on them psychologically.

Androcentrism is unspiritual because it ignores the spiritual value of the other half of the human race; it is immoral because it exploits the rest of creation. And it is un-Christian because it fails to find God incarnate in everything. That is why feminism denies the universalization of male experience. Women know that they see differently, too, and they want that vision honored for the sake of the human race. Women know that they think and feel differently about many things, and they want those thoughts and feelings factored into decisions—for the sake of the human race. Women know that they are different physically and they want their bodies valued, honored, and listened to in all the questions that affect life (not simply the biological ones) for the sake of the human race.

Feminism rejects hierarchy and domination, not for itself alone, but for the sake of the rest of the human race. In fact, ecofeminism—a feminism that integrates Genesis 2, science and ecology and the fullness of humanity—reconceives feminism itself. An equal rights feminism that simply wants what men have already is not enough. A radical feminism that seeks separatism and divides the human race on the pretext of bettering it is not enough. A socialist feminism that concentrates on what is good for humans but takes no account of nature is not enough.

Feminism—real feminism—is a new worldview that transcends male chauvinism, rejects female chauvinism, is not just anthropocentric, but embraces creation and rejoices in nature and sees the "image of God" in equal grandeur in both female and male, in the cosmos and the totality of creation.

Ecofeminism is a new worldview. Ecofeminism does not patronize and call that equality. Ecofeminism does not enslave and call that "God's will." Ecofeminism does not divide and call that liberation. Ecofeminism does not exclude and call that "the natural law."

Ecofeminism brings humanity to wholeness, wholeness to religion, and integrity to science.

Obviously, ecofeminism is not rebellion, not infidelity, not male-bashing, not female narcissism. It is simply the spiritual culmination that comes with the scientific awareness that life is not a ladder, that life is a weave of differences in concert.

The sin of racism, the sin of genocide, the destruction of the globe in the name of God and money, and the discord of sexism—however justified, however maintained—begin to pale when Genesis 1, the stewardship story, is forced to intersect with Genesis 2, the companionship story.

It is an awareness that is deep in the human heart, this awareness of connectedness. It is at the base of every revolution. It is the climax of consciousness that fueled the democratic revolutions of the eighteenth century, the Emancipation and Suffrage movements of the nineteenth century, the Endangered Species Act of 1973, the animal rights legislation of the 1990s, the rise of liberation theology, and the perdurance of feminism itself.

It cries out loud for a new way of thinking and seeing: it calls us to realize that autonomy is an illusion, that rationality is an insufficient measure of value, that women are no closer to nature than men and men are no further removed from nature than women, that dominion is destructive of the self, and that the human is called cultivator of everything God called "good."

We must begin to challenge the inhuman treatment of the nonhuman. We must refuse to see sexism as a theological given. We must see ourselves as part of nature, not outside of it. We must begin to see God in nature even while above it—as Trinity, as Sophia, as Mystery—rather than the kind of power that claims to make our misuse of power holy.

Religion itself must take responsibility for our irresponsibility. We are here to become, not to destroy.

One day the Buddha was threatened with death by a bandit on the road. "First," the Buddha said to the bandit, "honor my last wish and cut the branch off that tree." "There," the bandit said, handing the branch to the Buddha, "whatever good it will do you now." "Correct," said the Buddha. "So please put the branch back on the tree again." "You must be insane," the bandit said, "to think anyone could do that." "Oh, on the contrary, my friend," the Buddha said. "It is you who are insane if you think you are mighty simply because you can wound and destroy. The mighty are those who spend their strength to create and to heal."

"Saints do not see things others do not see," as Edwards wrote. "They see just what everyone else sees—but they see it differently."

We must begin to see that domination is the way of the weak. But our world—our entire world, with all its colors, all its women and men, its plants and animals—has need of empowerment now. We must begin to see differently if we really want to be holy.

We must begin, all of us, to put the tree of life back together again.

# Sanctity

"Saintliness," Jean Anouilh wrote in *Becket*, "is also a temptation." The truth of the insight simmers in the center of the soul. Or perhaps it should. The gnawing inclination to affect sanctity by pious gestures, the possibility of being seduced by false forms of sanctity, the allure of plastic saints who parade across the stages of our lives wrapped in incense and holy clothing while the world stays steeped in pain, expose the horrors of the "temptation to saintliness."

The Catholic tradition gives clear warning, strong models of a sanctity far beyond either the ethereal or the ascetic presentation of the self. Christian sanctity requires conversion to the will of God, immersion in the spirit of Jesus, and commitment to the human community. It calls us to wrestle with the self, to take on the searing audacity of Christ, and to give ourselves for the sake of the world around us. Christian sanctity is not the living of the law, it is the living of the life of the Jesus who walked the roads of Galilee feeding, curing, healing, and contending everywhere that he had come to bring the Reign of God. Its model is the Jesus who answered John's "Are you the one who is to come?" with "Go and tell John what you hear and see: the blind receive their sight, the lame walk, the lepers are cleansed, the deaf hear, the dead are raised, and the poor have good news brought to them" (Mt. 11:4–6). Clearly, the Christian does not go to heaven alone. When the holiness of some of us is built on the invisibility of the rest of us, good honest sin, artless self-centeredness, looks better than pseudo-saintliness.

Christian tradition makes the point painfully clear. We do not go to heaven by our own merit. We do not go to the heights of Christian spiritual development by preening our souls on ritual and holding ourselves above the fray of the human condition. On the contrary. The Christian saint is the one who has put on the mind of Christ and so put on the broken heart of the world. Such are the people whose sanctity challenges the lives of the rest of us.

The notion occurs that what we may be tempted to spend our lives doing in the name of sanctity may not be worth doing at all. We may set out to be exactly what the world does not need and what Jesus would disdain as the mark of "a whited sepulchre." That kind of sanctity is a snare of immense proportions for the sincere and the swindlers alike. For the sincere it poses the specter of a wasted life; for the swindler it threatens exposure. On the one hand, to seek sanctity in the wrong places is to risk an empty soul. To assume that regularity of devotions and rigor of discipline is the stuff of sanctity is to assume that we can make gods of ourselves for ourselves by ourselves. This is sanctity untested. On the other hand, to pretend sanctity for the wrong reasons is to guarantee a distorted soul. To posture in front of the human race, without substance, without benefit of tempering, without the currency of human significance as basis of exchange, is to twist the fibers of our lives into a tapestry of nothing. Sincere as it may be in its excesses, enticing as it may be in its public allure, false sanctity—sanctity steeped in the self—is not Christian. Sanctity must be for something beyond the satisfaction of the self, beyond a kind of protective piety or a bid for public approval.

When we set out to be holy in the Christian tradition, then, what exactly are we setting out to do and how shall we know it if we see it?

Styles of sanctity mark every period of Christian history, some of them startlingly simple, some of them verging on the neurotic. Christian sanctity has ranged from both total negation of life and total proclamation of the Word. Choosing one from the other is the central spiritual challenge of every age. It has both personal and public meaning. Whatever its particular form in any given culture, the real saint has always been considered as much public witness as private devotee. Those were saints who touched the lives of others in significant ways as well as concentrated on their own.

The Christian saint becomes the Face of God at the center point of life, reminding each of us that we are called to do more than exist and to be more than a breath lost in the night of time. What we take as the models of our own lives, then, not only changes us but turns our entire world around one degree at a time. Sanctity is not a private devotion. The summons to sanctity is an invitation to choose carefully the way we spend our souls, to choose for the gospel rather than for the sense of the perfect self, or the preservation of the perfect institution, or even for the security of a very banal salvation.

Christian sanctity is greater than the self, larger than private piety, more meaningful than religion for its own sake. It is no single state of life, no single work, no particular set of circumstances. It is as diverse as a Judean desert, a wedding feast in Cana, a temple in Jerusalem. The best of Christian tradition finds its saints in crowds as well as in hermitages, on mountaintops as well as in caves, at the resurrection as well as at the foot of the cross, in the noisy as well as the quiet, in women who defy the system to build a better world and in men who give their lives so that others may have life "and have it more abundantly."

What the world calls saints, what "saints" call sanctity, says something to the rest of us about what our own lives can be. All of them bring to consciousness the notion that there may be far more to life than we are seeing. There may be far more in life than what we have managed to acquire. There may be far more that life demands of us than we are willing to give. Christian sanctity is clearly more a communal than a private concept, more a social than a personal process. What I am, the rest of the world has the right to be. What I am becomes benchmark for the rest of society as well. I carry on my back the obligation to be what the world needs me to be, and I look in hope for those who have carried that same obligation before me. The Christian life requires a commitment to the life of the Christ who consorted with sinners, cured lepers, raised women from the dead, contested with the officials, and challenged the state. It is a life of prophetic presence and selfless service in a world whose soul has gone dry.

Saints, as a result, have always been a part of Christian history. They are those who, clear of soul and straight of eye, chart their lives by remembering its meaning. Saints mark the way for those who come after them. They are the pathfinders, the models, the stars in the darkness of every generation who enable us to remember the glory of humanity as well as the magnetism of divinity. They give us promise of possibility in the depths of despair and hope in the midst of the mundane. They bring new light to those parts of life grown dull from neglect. They remind us at our worst of what humanity can be at its best. They give us new insight into old truths, a new look at the God in our midst who goes among us so that "the blind may see and the deaf may hear and the poor may have proof of liberation."

Saints have been used and misused, undervalued and overlooked, misunderstood and overrated in every generation. Some have been called "saint" in one generation and ignored in the next. Some have been underestimated in one time and overemphasized in another. But most have simply been the memory of the human race for greatness of spirit. Most have been simple people who, when thrust into situations of public meaning, responded out of deep personal spirituality. The Sufi tell of the disciple who asked the elder, "Is there anything I can do to make myself enlightened?" "As little as you can do to make the sun rise in the morning." "Then, of what use are the spiritual exercises you prescribe?" "To make sure you are not asleep when the sun begins to rise."

Christian devotion is nothing more than preparation for Christian sanctity. It cultivates the soul so that when the moment for holy presence finally becomes imperative, we will have been prepared to grasp and grip and seize it. Christian sanctity is a great deal more than Christian devotion. Christian sanctity requires that we become what we seek so that others, in their own moments of spiritual contest, can have the comfort of it, too.

For those who ask, then, Why have saints? the answer is, Why not have saints? Every generation needs heroes. It is not that saints are humans who have become divine. It is that saints are humans who have become fully human, fully the best that a human can be, fully attuned to life at its most meaningful. The saints are those around us in tiny neighborhoods and spacious offices who confront us daily with the great questions of life and bring to them the answer of themselves.

We search for the signs of the best in ourselves at all times and in all places. We measure ourselves by the measure of those who have wrestled with the same angels, lived in the same darkness, borne the same heat of the day and come to triumph, come to light, come to a new consciousness of the truth of life despite the pressures around them and the struggles within. We look for those around us who make life's great Jesus-story real and true. We watch for those who have touched Jesus and become new because of it so that we ourselves can find purpose in stretching to touch it.

The problem with defining saints is the problem of defining standards. Who is to say what "sanctity" really is? In fact, can anyone else but me begin to know what I have been through in life and with what honor, what depth, what nobility? Can anyone know whether I have survived it with more or less valor, with more or less faith? Can anyone know what I have borne to be my best self? And does anyone really do it without struggle? They are questions of phenomenal import. St. Therese of Lisieux, whose papers were sanitized by her community for public consumption, was made to look to the world like putty in the hands of God. In the last days of her life, however, she writes in her personal journal, "I am assailed by the worst temptations of atheism." Clearly, lack of struggle is not of the essence of sanctity. It is struggling that makes for sanctity.

For centuries the church has confronted the human community with role models of greatness. We call them saints when what we really often mean to say is "icon," "star," "hero"—ones so possessed by an internal vision of divine goodness that they give us a glimpse of the face of God in the center of the human. They give us a taste of the possibilities of greatness in ourselves.

But sadly, two things have happened to the modern notion of saint: first, saints have become official; second, saints have become bland.

In the fourteenth century, after hundreds of years of identification of saints by popular acclaim, the Vatican developed a process and criteria to determine if the persons venerated by a local population were worthy of general emulation. The canonization process, for the most part, had both substance and merit. The proliferation of local saints by the people who knew them or were impressed by the fruits of their spirituality or the value of their works was a grand and perceptive gesture. If nothing else, it has something to teach us about becoming aware of the character of those around us, those standing beside us today, bringing the white heat of the gospel to the ordinariness of the circumstances. Nevertheless, this redundancy of good served as much to blur the character of greatness as it did to preserve its image. "Saints" sprang up everywhere as every area, every region, every city, every village scrambled for relics and patrons.

At the same time, an officially constructed canonization process separated the people in need of models from the very personalities and forces that had given spirit to their lives in the here and now. In most cases, only those reputations that lasted far beyond the life of the person nominated for sainthood were seen as fit for examination by the Congregation for the Causes of Saints. By that time, of course, their spiritual fame had often waned, their social influence dimmed.

The canonization process looked for the heroic in the good; separated the merely pious from the powerfully holy; wanted miracles as well as the proof of a good life to qualify a person for canonization; concentrated on professional religious figures to the prejudice of lay people, and men to the detriment of women, the rich rather than the poor; concentrated on ecclesiastical docility as a sign of holiness; and judged cases according to the insights of centuries sometimes far removed.

To this day, the process keeps popular hysteria from becoming the norm of holiness. It also runs the risk, however, of reducing holy passion to the level of prosaic piety. It hazards sanctifying the insipid. It chances turning goodness into cardboard. It disqualifies from consideration people who fall in the course of rising to new human heights. It cuts holiness from a common cloth: the theologically proper, the ecclesiastically docile, the morally safe. As a result, it eliminates from regard an entire body of people because of whom the very soul of the world has been stretched but who may not be synchronous with the current ideas of the church, who may not even be Catholic, who may not be without signs of flaw and struggle. It leads, imperceptibly but almost invariably, to a theology of disillusionment, the notion that only the perfect, the Christian, give us glimpses of the face of God— Moses and Abraham, the Samaritan woman and Peter, David and Samson to the contrary.

Clearly not everyone who points the way to God for us may themselves be perfect. There are figures gleaming in their holy causes who are awkward in their personal lives. They are sometimes in confusion, as we are. They are often in conflict with themselves, as we are. They are virtuous beyond telling in one dimension and weak to the point of sin in others. At the same time, they hold a fire in their hearts bright enough to light a way for many. They are impelled by the will of God for humankind, and they will brook no less. They stand on gilded stilts above the rest of their generation, their comrades, their kind and become a sign for all generations. They are a proof of possibility from ages past and a symbol of hope for ages yet to come. They stand in mute conviction of the age in which they live and challenge us to do the same. Most of all, they are important to us now. "One does not help only one's own generation," the Hasidim teach. "Generation after generation, David pours enthusiasm into somber souls; generation after generation, Samson arms weak souls with the strength of heroes."

Sanctity in the Christian tradition requires far more than personal piety, then. It assumes a life so rooted in the will of God, so committed to others, and so large in the scope of its concerns that it raises questions in the hearts of the rest of us about the quality of our own souls, the depth of our own lives, the value of our own choices. The saint confronts us with the heart of Jesus and the mind of God. The saint takes our breath away. We see in them what we know that we ourselves should be and hang our heads, not in shame but in contemplation. The saint does not preach platitudes; the saint cries justice and gives service until justice comes.

Christian sanctity requires public commitment more than personal piety, as important as piety is for the cultivation of the Christian soul.

Christian sanctity goes beyond the incarnation to the crucifixion, beyond presence to the other to the point of being willing to suffer for the other.

Christian sanctity holds up for all to see the standards of the gospel in a world that prefers charity to justice.

Christian sanctity brings each of us to our knees before the questions of the soul, challenges each of us to measure ourselves against a canon higher than our own, shows each of us the way beyond ourselves to others, beyond goodness to the gospel, beyond private and parochial concerns to cosmic commitment.

The saint sees the world as God sees the world and responds wherever they are, however they must, so that the Jesus who lives in them may live through them.

It is a dark and dangerous journey and means more than a fidelity to dogma, more than the preservation of doctrine, more than the keeping of the law. It demands high valor and great faith.

It lives hidden sometimes, as Charles de Foucauld did with the Arabs simply to build a private bridge between Islam and Christianity. It becomes hugely public sometimes, as did Bartolomé de Las Casas in his defense of the humanity of the American Indians. It goes where it may not go and does what it may not do, as did Catherine of Siena in her involvement in church politics and her criticism of the pope. It lives a fiercely abandoned life sometimes, as did Franz Jägerstätter who alone of all his village refused induction into Hitler's army and was executed because of it. But always, always, it lives more out of principle than it does out of piety. It goes above and beyond the normal norms to show again God's glory waiting in the normal. It lives the daily in a way that challenges us all. And it is in no way amenable to the official standards of the day. Francis of Assisi stretched the mind of the church about wealth. Teresa of Avila expanded the vision of the church about the nature of private spirituality. Harriet Tubman taught the church in her courageous deceit what it could be in the face of fear. Monsignor Hugh O'Flaherty, Vatican official in World War II Rome, proved in his protection of Jewish refugees that the church was still capable of sanctity in a world full of sin.

Some hear the call to the demands of dailiness. Some prefer instead to make dailiness the excuse for not listening to the demands it really makes, for choosing piety rather than sanctity. Indeed, "Saintliness is also a temptation." Indeed, saintliness can be its own sin, in which case we must learn to repent the private little nests we have made for ourselves in the name of the spiritual life. We must begin once again to walk the roads of Galilee with the One who brings us into ourselves to wrestle with the demons designed to keep us there, beyond ourselves to a world in need, and above ourselves to see the world as God sees the world. We must become what we all think we cannot be if we are ever to become what we are all called to be: "icons," "rebels," "stars," and "saints."

# Tradition

~~~~~~~~

*T* here's an ancient story that bears retelling, perhaps, in an age of discrimination, refugees, planned destruction of the planet, government lies, and the industrialized slavery of the Third World.

Once upon a time, the story goes, a disciple said to the elder, "Holy One, I have a great spiritual question to ask. Is there life after death?" And the Holy One answered: "Ah, that is an interesting question, but it is not the greatest of spiritual questions. The greatest of spiritual questions is, Is there life before death?"

A second imperative from scripture is related to the first. The Book of Proverbs teaches: "Lead a child up in the way they must go and when they are old they will not depart from the way."

Jesus was devoted to life before death, and Jesus was formed in it from childhood. If we want life before death, we will have to be developed in the same way.

Most of the Catholics of my generation were formed in the catechism; religion was reduced to absolutes and laws, to lists of sins and lists of Holy Days of Obligation, to theological formulas and personal devotions, to legalism and pietism. Religion was a private matter; individualism was the high priest of the New World, and "the white man's burden" was the bedrock of foreign policy.

No wonder we grew up looking so different from the Jesus who said, "Feed my sheep," and the Jesus who rose to return, not to Jerusalem—the center of power—but to Galilee, the backwater of Israel where the poor and the outcast, the illiterate and the unwanted, the simple and the unsophisticated were waiting for deliverance. Jesus, you see, was not raised on the catechism. Jesus was raised on the psalms.

Sung for centuries, the psalms have captured the spiritual wisdom and insights of one generation after another. They sing of praise and fear and faith and final victory. They sing all the human emotions to God. They talk to God. They scour the world for answers to the unanswerable. They ring across time with the human memory of the fidelity of God and the soul searching of humanity and the highest aspirations and the deepest pain of the human soul. They sing of a theology of human life that transcends national boundaries and personal privatism and private profitism. They sing of the whole human race united in the God who is life. They sing of a people who sin as a people and are saved as a people and sigh for God as a people and see God everywhere. The psalms are a crash course in justice, not a compendium of laws. The psalms called Jesus beyond Judaism and stretch us still beyond ourselves.

It is impossible to pray the psalms and settle for parochialism. It is inconceivable to pray the psalms and foster national chauvinism. It is unthinkable to pray the psalms and wallow in a theology of domination that gives some of us the right to misuse the rest of us in the name of capitalism or communism or clericalism or sexism or racism or arrogance.

And Jesus was aware of that because Jesus prayed the psalms as a way of life.

What did Jesus learn in the psalms that we theologize about, perhaps, but take more as questions than as answers?

Jesus learned that the poor are heard. "You listen to the needy and the oppressed," Psalm 69 declares. "When the poor cry to me

I will hear them," Psalm 34 insists. It is a dire warning for those with ears to hear. The psalms do not say that the poor will be miraculously saved. Oh, no. The psalms simply promise that the poor will be heard. And remembered, presumably. And vindicated in the end. Like Lazarus with Dives.

The psalms imply quite forthrightly that though you and I may not hear the poor, God will. Eventually. When it counts. And you and I who do not hear them and stoop down to them and reach out to them and stand up for them will ourselves go unheard on the side of God's deaf ear.

And so Jesus, formed in the psalms, heard the poor on the Sabbath and in the temple and at the tables of the rich.

The question for our time is whether or not we, too, speak for the poor of our worlds—for the blacks who are being deprived of their culture in the name of Catholicism while Anglos and Europeans have it aplenty; for the women who are being told that Jesus's message to them is, "Don't follow me"; for the theologians who are attempting to ask new questions so that the gospel can be relevant to a new age; and for the poor of the world in every corner, every country of our world who are left out of a capitalist equation in which weakness is not acceptable and people are expendable.

Jesus learned in the psalms that the world is a cosmic reality, not a local and nationalistic preserve of the chosen few. "The creator loves all the children of earth and shapes the hearts of each," Psalm 33 reminds us. God's blessing rains on all, in other words. "God touches all in the heavens and on earth," Jesus was constantly reminded. "Everything is full of sacred presence," he heard in Psalm 103. In the face of the unseeing and the uncaring, Jesus learned that the planet is not ours for the exploiting. The universe is not ours for the controlling. The people are not ours for the enslaving. God gives good and wants good for everyone.

Jesus, it is clear, blessed Jew and non-Jew alike, the centurion and the Samaritan, the woman as well as the man, the world's unjust as well as the just. In God, the psalms say to a world of debutante balls and closed clubs and "undeveloped" peoples, there are simply no standards, no status qualifications, no people with whom we associate in contrast to those with whom we do not, no nations less bright, less human, less deserving of the fruits of humankind than we are.

Yet we take our factories into the Third World and decide the level at which those people may live. Indeed, we export our industries but not our wage scales or our pension plans or our labor standards or our health benefits and say that we have done a good thing. "Where would those people be without our industry?" we argue and buy caftans in the Philippines for $7.00 each and sell them in Florida for $70.00 apiece. And we pride ourselves on the fact that we ended the slavery system that provided our domestic labor with a house and a family network so that today we can pay slave wages and not be required to provide the house and food for the slave family. It is a spirituality that is far removed from the psalms that cried out for justice to the widow, the orphan, and the foreigner, for recognition of the sacred presence in all.

What Jesus learned in Psalm 145 is that God is the God of all. "All creatures look to you with hope," Jesus learned to pray, "and you sustain them in their need. You are generous to all creation, nourishing all who live." And Jesus taught Samaritans and cured pagans and talked to Romans and taught women, whom Jews disdained in the public arena, some very public things. It was to women, in fact, that Jesus first taught the fact that he was the Messiah and that he was risen from the dead.

Discrimination in the name of religion, in other words, is a heinous thing. A crusade against Arabs and a holocaust of Jews have no place in the lives of a psalmic people. The obliteration of the Romans and the neglect of the Samaritans have no rank in the mind of those who have begun to see the world through the filter of the psalms. The nuclear disintegration of the planet is simply unthinkable to a psalmic people. The exploitation of the globe is lunatic to a psalmic people. The feminization of poverty is unimaginable to a psalmic people. The denigration and disenfranchisement and theological erasure of women are simply unacceptable to a people who pray the psalms and understand the psalms and grow in the spirituality of the psalms.

"Vengeance is mine; I shall repay," Jesus learned from the psalms. "The power of the wicked shall be broken. God takes care of the just," Jesus breathed over and over again in Psalm 37. And surely the concept was comforting when he faced the hostile rabbis and the scornful soldiers and the manipulated witnesses. But in a search for false peace, we have perhaps forgotten the energy that comes from knowing holy anger and leaving the results to God.

There have been movements, even in the monastic prayer tradition, that are based squarely in the center of the psalms, to eliminate what have come to be called the "Cursing Psalms." "What place does cursing have in prayer?" the purists argue. But perhaps the better question is, Where else shall we take our curses than to prayer where we acknowledge at the time of our deepest pain that punishment does not belong to us, that God is the God of justice? How else do we explain that Jesus went "like a lamb to slaughter," not without struggle, but without meanness, because Jesus knew that whatever the price of his own commitment, God would in the end do it justice? How else do we account for the fact that Jesus does not call down the hosts of heaven even in his own behalf or allow Peter to take up the sword? How else do we explain the fact that Jesus saw sin and did not punish it, saw pain and did not condone it, saw truth and did not flinch from it?

But we revel in those who take justice into their own hands and take preeminence to ourselves and take racism as the will of God and take sexism as natural. Abraham Lincoln pointed out to those who prayed that the North would win the Civil War that it did not matter whether or not God was on our side but what mattered was simply whether or not we were on God's side. That was a psalmic mentality far removed from a period of messianic Americanism. We can invade a country and displace its people and gerrymander its government in the name of our own justice. We can suspend the principles of the Constitution as long as we are not on American territory, the Supreme Court has ruled. We can, apparently, usurp and exploit and undermine for our own brand of truth and justice as long as it is in the interest of the USA, no matter who is hurt or who is forgotten or who is destroyed and call ourselves a religious people and everyone else pagan. But that is not the psalmic mentality of Jesus to whom Samaritans are worth saving and women are worth raising from the dead and Romans are worth obeying.

"Uphold my cause, O God, for I walk in integrity. I trust in you. I shall stand firm," Jesus prayed in Psalm 26. Trust, indeed, became the cornerstone of a Jesus who was not received by those to whom he was sent and rejected by those whom he had healed and misunderstood by those to whom he had explained himself. Trust became what drove him on and kept him certain in the face of confusion and failure and disinterest. It is trust that we, too, must learn if our own lives are to have purpose and constancy in the midst of fatigue. How does anyone go on in the peace movement or the woman's issue or the justice questions who does not trust that a better heart than the hearts that rule the systems and write the laws and share the wealth will ultimately gain the day? The Jesus who trusted all the way to Calvary is the Jesus who asks us to trust as well. But trust is not a virtue until there is reason to despair. This psalmic people who knew slavery and ex-ile and siege and destruction taught the world to trust. And in Jesus came the clearest sign of it.

Indeed the mind of Jesus has been formed very differently from ours. Obviously, the psalms outdo the boundaries of the catechism and the provincialism of a nation and the narrowness of bigots.

"Let those who hope in you not be put to shame through me, God of Hosts," Jesus prayed in Psalm 69.

"Let not those who seek you be dismayed through me, God of Israel," Jesus learned. No one, in other words, should see in us anything that makes them doubt the authenticity of the Christian revelation, that God lives in us. People should be able to see in us what our God is like. Whatever we do, we do as sign to others of the continuing presence of a caring, courageous Christ. That's what being Christian is all about. That's what it is to be formed in the psalms, as Jesus was.

Advocacy, creationism, universalism, justice, trust and witness are what Jesus learned in the psalms and lived when he cured on the Sabbath and modeled when he touched the doubly polluted corpse of the woman and witnessed to when he listened to the poor and risked when he disputed with the rabbis in the temple. It is, to this day, the legacy of the psalms. Maybe that's why a domesticated people are less inclined to pray them now.

Prayer, of course, is not meant to be a magic act that cajoles and coaxes God to turn life into a Disneyland of religion. Prayer is not meant to change the world; prayer is meant to change us so that we will then change the world.

Jesus, clearly, had learned to pray. The question for our time is, Have we? We know how to worry, we know how to beg, we know how to fantasize in prayer, we know how to make prayer an escape. But we will not be praying until we have become immersed in the mind and presence of God, as Jesus was; until we have come to see God everywhere, in everyone; until we have come to listen to the poor; until we have come to work as God would work in this world; until we have come to give our wrath over to the wrath of God; until we have come to trust and trust and trust that somehow, someday what must happen will happen because we have added our part to it.

As he walks the dry and dusty roads of Galilee with the poor and unsophisticated, we see how the psalms have formed Jesus. As he debates the doctrines of law with the doctors of the church who have shaped the possibilities of God to themselves, we see how the psalms have formed Jesus. As he gives people more care and attention than he does institutions, we see how the psalms have formed Jesus. As we see his nondenominationalism, his awareness of God everywhere, in everyone, we see how the psalms have formed Jesus.

The question is, then, What is forming us? When the papers point out that we are deporting the poor from the richest nation in the world, we must ask what is forming us. When we maximize our profits at the expense of others, we must ask what is forming us. When we name some peoples expendable or ignorable, or uneducable, we must ask what is forming us. When we swallow our holy angers for the sake of a plastic peace or strike out to destroy what is not yet like us, we must ask what is forming us. When we forget that there is injustice in the world because the just do nothing about it, we must ask what is forming us. When we despair of God's grace or God's presence or God's consuming and ultimate justice, we must ask what adolescent, magical, superficial, and fanciful notions of God are forming us.

Jesus pronounced his own formation directly. "I have come that they may have life and have it more abundantly," he declared. "The great spiritual question," the Holy One said, "is not whether or not there is life after death. The great spiritual question is whether or not there is life before death."

Those are the fruits of real spiritual formation. To have life and to give life, now and overflowing. Those are the ideas that formed Jesus, and those are the convictions, if we are ever to be truly Christian, that must someday form us.

# Equality

There is an old tale that may describe best the role of women in the Roman Catholic Church today.

In a Buddhist monastery in the Far East, the story tells, twenty monks and one nun, whose name was Eshun, were practicing meditation with a certain Zen master.

Eshun was very attractive and very holy, and several of the monks fell secretly in love with her. One of them even wrote her a love letter, insisting upon a private meeting. But Eshun did not reply.

The following day the master gave a lecture to the group, and when it was over Eshun arose. Addressing the one who had written her, she said, "If you really love me so much, come and embrace me now."

The situation for women in the Roman Catholic Church today is, it seems, not all too different from Eshun's. Catholic women presumably are also loved, written glowingly about in fact, approached often in secret by clerics and bishops of all sorts who encourage their efforts in the woman's movement and doubt the value of the present practices of the church. Seldom, however, are women officially recognized and never, never are they formally embraced by the church in public: there are no women at the altar, no women in the Cardinalate, no women prefects of curial offices, no women expected in liturgical processions or as spiritual directors in seminaries or as the anointers of the dying whom they catechized.

We have reached the stage in the church obviously where women are to be heard but not seen. And that's the good news.

It has been much more in the character of the tradition for women not to be heard either. For centuries, and right up to our own time, women have been talked about only as sinners or as children, if they were talked about at all. The 1917 Code of Canon Law referred to women directly only once, for instance, and then only to say that "certain persons have a necessary legal domicile; a married woman the domicile of her husband, a minor the domicile of the parent; an insane person, that of his guardian" (c. 93).

For the most part women were simply defined as morally threatening and intellectually inferior. Men, in fact, were cautioned to keep them at a distance, not out of concern for their own male weakness, but out of fear of the woman's wiles. John Chrysostom makes the inherent evil of women clear in his "On Priesthood." He writes:

"There are in the world a great many situations that weaken the conscientiousness of the soul. First and foremost of these is dealings with women. In his concern for the male sex, the superior may not forget the females, who need greater care precisely because of their ready inclination to sin. In this situation the evil enemy can find many ways to creep in secretly. For the eye of woman touches and disturbs our soul, and not only the eye of the unbridled woman, but that of the decent one as well" (VI, CH. 8). He brooks no exception from the law.

"The whole sex is weak and flighty," he says. "What then, is there no salvation for them?" he asks. "Yes, there is," he says. "What kind? Salvation through children" (Ninth Homily on I Tim. 2:15).

As a result of teachings like these, normative in their content and universal in their application, laws were written to restrain women, and books were written to guide them as good wives and mothers, the one arena acknowledged to be natural to them. Childbearing and childbearing alone became their role, not because childbearing was seen as woman's necessarily beautiful and spiritually creative contribution to the development of humanity but because women were seen as too bad for anything else, a totally carnal being in a world where flesh and spirit were at bitter conflict.

As a result, women were kept out of the sanctuary, out of the schools and out of the public domain. And all in the name of God. And for centuries and centuries.

The honest fact is, however, that things are not nearly as bad now as they were in my grandmother's time. The fact is, also, that things are not nearly as good now as they should be.

In my own lifetime, in the last fifty years in fact, there have been changes of monumental importance wrapped in tiny, trivial packages. Both women and men, for instance, are permitted to sing in church choirs now, a task once reserved only to men and small boys with soprano voices.

The Churching Ceremony, which readmitted a woman to the church after childbirth in a manner reminiscent of the Jewish purification ceremony, has been abandoned and with it the feeling of banishment that came with doing the only thing that men said a woman was made for, giving birth.

Women are finally permitted to read the scriptures out loud and from inside the sanctuary of the church, a sign if there ever was one that they are a woman's scriptures, too.

Women can touch the vessels of the altar, a privilege once accorded to eleven-year-old altar boys but not to their mothers.

And in the wake of those breakthroughs, there are at least a few women chancellors and women department heads and women consultants to diocesan boards and women administrators of parishes and women judges on marriage tribunals.

There are a growing number of parishes who even encourage the presence of female altar servers and some make room, at least on special occasions, for women homilists—many of whom are better prepared theologically for the job than the regular parish priest. A few even change the male language of the hymns that trumpet "men's salvation" for all the women of the world to hear and to decide if this time the word really includes them or not.

The bishops themselves, in fact, have called for the elimination of sexist language in the reading of scripture to recognize that the Covenant is meant for women, too. We talk about "sons and daughters" now rather than simply the "sons" of God. Indeed there have been gains. Great gains.

Women now are routinely granted degrees in theology, the sole and private preserve of male clerics until the late 1940s because it was a "sacred" subject and so out of the province of women.

The bishops have written a document, unpublished true, but written at least, which at long last and after millions of pious women submitted to the brutality of "the will of God for them" admits—declares indeed—that sexism is a sin and that wife-beating is immoral.

Make no doubt about it, there has been progress: minds have changed, attitudes are shifting, some behaviors are being corrected, expectations are high. The unthinkable, that women may be full human beings with all that implies theologically and socially, has become thinkable apparently.

To deny the progress of these times is not only to be unfair, it is to deny the very possibility of progress. If we forget where we have come from, it may be impossible to maintain the energy it will take to get where we are going.

So, it is extremely important, I think, to remember aloud and always that once, and in this very generation in fact, we truly believed and passively accepted the notion that, since church music had been defined as a liturgical act, it was reserved for clerics and their male substitutes and that it was liturgically impossible, sacramentally deficient for women to sing in the church.

It is purposeful to remember that once not long ago we bowed quietly to the notion that no woman except, of course, a sacristan with mop in hand was allowed in the sanctuary because the sanctuary of God was a male domain where God did not want women, except as servants, of course.

It is functional to remember that though only some fifty years ago women were denied degrees in theology, that in the year 2001 women received 19 percent of the doctoral degrees, 40 percent of the masters degrees, and 18 percent of the bachelors degrees in theology that were awarded in the United States alone.

In the light of such changes from the mundane to the momentous, it is essential to ask what there is now that we passively accept and docilely bear as God's will for women that is changeable, that must be changed, if the church is to be church.

The point is that because women have some rights now that they did not have before, it is easier to contend and clearer to see that they should have all of them. When the immutables became mutable, the church and the world may indeed have changed, but they clearly did not end as some supposed, and a lot of people have profited from the changing of them, men as well as women.

With the expectation that women, too, will be self-directed adults, we have men now who are liberated from the burden of playing God: to have to be all-knowing and all-powerful when a person needs and feels weak can lead either to tyranny or to breakdown. With admission to the adult world, we have women with higher self-esteem and less mental illness because they are finally being allowed to develop and encouraged to participate in the public dimensions of life. With the education of women, we have teachers of religion now who are grounded as well in theology as they are in piety. With the routine presence of women on church boards and planning committees, we have another whole dimension of spiritual and social life being expressed at the centers of the parishes. With the acknowledgment that women, too, have spiritual insights and theological creativity, we have the beginning of the expression of a feminine spirituality and a feminist theology that is both critique and call to traditional constructs. With the development of feminist exegesis, we have a richer reading of scripture and a freer expression of liturgy. With a church that is becoming both male and female—theologically, liturgically, pastorally—we have the beginnings of a celebrating human family.

We are a richer people for it, and that new richness must be recognized, admitted, and celebrated.

But there is a great deal that women do not have as yet, as well. Like Eshun, women get love but they get little respect. Women are made exceptions to in the church instead of the measure of its wholeness and authenticity. Indeed now, there is almost always one woman on every church committee, one woman on every theological panel, one woman on every parish staff. But there are seldom balanced numbers of them. They are tokens, in other words, and tokenism is not theological development. Tokenism is commitment to a theology of deviance.

The problem with tokenism is that it takes a few outsiders into the center of the system in order to keep the rest of the population out and make the system look good at the same time. The problem with tokenism is that nothing really changes. The system stays the same: the powerful are still powerful; the outsiders are still outsiders; the norm is still the norm. The tokens on the parish councils and episcopal committees become the window dressing on the religion, but not a clearly substantial and essential part of any diocese, any parish, any church enterprise, any theological deliberation. The new look is paraded and applauded, but the old theology remains operational. It is men who bless them and shrive them and judge them and tell them what God wants of women since God, apparently, does not deign to deal with women directly, all the saints and mystics of the church to the contrary, all Marian theology aside.

It is men, after all, who make the exceptions that allow all the token women of the world to attend their meetings. There is no decree, no requirement, no right that is being honored. The world stays securely the same. It is men who make the rules and men who have the power to take them away.

Clearly, a great deal more will have to change before we will be able to tell with certainty that God decided to "make them in God's own image," and so "male and female God made them."

Some important dimensions are lacking, without which we

will be very unlikely to progress beyond the sterile, the safe, and the secure in the question of the role of the women in the church. And never to the holy.

The spiritual concept of God must be reclaimed.

The continuing emphasis on God as Father rather than on God as Spirit, as Life, as Essence, as all Being is very subtly limiting of women and very clearly controlling of them. If God is male, then males are, indeed, closer to God. Femaleness becomes the undivine other, the leftover, the unknown, the unholy, the addenda. And, of course, the subordinate. But even to hint at the possibility that the generation of life is an exclusively male prerogative by arguing that God must be seen as father because God is the generator of life is to participate in embarrassingly bad biology. It is, then, even worse theology. Heresy, perhaps.

Maleness, as a result, has become the new idolatry, the new golden calf which we worship in our churches and confirm in our social structures. Consequently, the feminine dimensions of God go unnoted and unknown in a world that has appropriated the warrior God to its militaristic self but has completely overlooked the birthing God who gives us all everything we need for life, if we will only distribute it.

We will certainly be what we worship. But we worship only half the reality of life. Of course God is a personal God. Of course God is father. But God is much more than that, as the language of the church has always maintained. We have traditionally called God rock, fire, dove, and lion. We must begin to ask ourselves, then, why we never, ever call God mother.

As long as our image of God remains so narrow, so will our experience of God in the world. So will our vision of church.

Sacramental theology must begin openly to challenge its inconsistencies and internal contradictions.

If baptism does indeed "make new creatures of us all," then why do only some of us get to grow to a full stature of this new creaturehood? If women are really equal in the image of God, then why are women denied sacramental access to God without the medium of a male? And why is it that we have wrenched the doctrine of "Incarnation" to the point that we prefer to believe that Jesus became male rather than that "the Word became flesh?"

If women are really "bone of my bone, flesh of my flesh," then they are surely equal if for no other reason than the DNA. Why, then, do we insist on the doctrine of complementarity rather than equality?

Why is it, in other words, that we say that women can get some graces, but not all graces? Why is it that women can receive grace, apparently, but never, ever dispense it?

The point is that our theologies of baptism, incarnation, grace, redemption, and Eucharist are askew, at war with themselves, incompatible. The point is that if grace is not gender-specific, then God may have absolutely outrageous plans for women that man-made institutions have no right to obstruct.

We are to believe that the God who would choose a woman to turn God into the body and blood of Christ never wants a woman to do the same with bread.

It is not what sexism says about women that is sinful. It is what sexism says about God that is wrong. Sexism really implies that God is all powerful—except when it comes to women, at which point the God who could draw water from a rock and raise the dead to life is totally powerless to work as fully through a woman as through a man. Indeed, have no doubt about it: It is God who is being held hostage to sexism and, as a result, the world.

The images of women must change.

Once the image of God is twisted and the image of grace is warped, it is only a small step away from the ruination of the image of woman herself. She becomes body but not brain, functionary but not force, child but not adult, creature but not person.

We have defined woman as "mother," but we have not defined man as "father." We have called woman "helpmate," but we have not called man "partner." We have defined woman as irrational and man as rational, an arrogance in the wake of the human history of holocaust and nuclearism and present technological warfare that boggles the mind. It is those very things, perhaps, that may prove the undoing of a people who have cut off half their human sensitivity.

It is time to realize that we need one another as persons, each-to-each a lesson, a call, and a model; each-to-each servant and helpmate and friend.

Has the woman's movement failed? Why aren't the young as vigorous in their pursuit of the woman's movement as their mothers and grandmothers had apparently been? Have we wasted our time? Have we done the wrong things? Is the heritage of the woman's movement a broken church, a disoriented society?

I've spent a lot of time thinking about those questions. As a result I began to ask questions of my own. One day, for instance, I simply went from office to office and reading station to reading station in a small college library and asked other women, young and old, "Is your life any different because of the woman's movement? And, if so, how?" The answers were at least provocative if not astounding.

Older women were quick to respond. In the last thirty years, one said, there is "a different attitude toward women. There's greater respect for their intelligence," but, she added, "there's still inequality of salaries, so I don't know how much of the respect is real yet."

The younger middle-aged woman beside her said, "Well, I'm not afraid of hitting them head-on now. If something's wrong, I don't take a back seat anymore. I was quiet, but when you see other women standing up for their rights, then you can, too. I'm a single parent. If you don't stand up, you're left with nothing." Then she lowered her voice a bit. "But the woman's movement is very hard for men," she said. "We know now that we can do almost anything, and men don't like that. Women have changed. They'll take power now."

One of the library assistants said, "We look at our children differently now. My daughters say, 'Mom, why didn't you play hockey when you were a child?' and I don't know how to tell them that we weren't allowed to do those things. No woman ran a marathon, and if they did let us play games like basketball they wrote girls' rules because they said we couldn't run the full court like the boys did. And we believed them," she said with a touch of both wistfulness and anger in her voice.

The woman checking the book out at the counter was very thoughtful for a moment. "Well, lots has changed but we still fall into stereotypes. In some ways it has worked to our disadvantage. Now women have to deal with new expectations, old roles, and triple the work."

"Oh, yes, my life is different as a result of the woman's movement," the secretary said. "Women get a lot more respect. They can go into different fields. They're taken seriously. And," she added with emphasis, "they can get out of bad situations." But then she thought for a moment. "There's just one thing," she said finally. "It's harder now for a woman to stay at home. In the first place, a family can't afford it. And now," she added, "the value of homemaking has just been lost."

It was the younger women, though, who left me with the most to consider. "What do I think about the woman's movement?" one of two young students said while she went right on filling out her registration forms. "Well, to tell you the truth I never really think about it at all. But if you ask, I think women are losing their femininity to it. I mean they're all so business oriented, and they don't want to have children."

"The woman's movement hasn't helped me at all," one of the employees behind the office counter said. "It just raised all the prices after women began to work so now everybody has to work to make up the money we lost when men started losing jobs to women."

"Just wait a minute," the second of the students said. "Personal development is important to human growth for women as well as for men. I know that a lot of the message of the woman's movement has been lost because of the style of the messenger, but we're forgetting something. Women have always worked. My mother worked. It's just that now I have choices that she never got. And it shouldn't be called the 'woman's movement' in the first place. Everyone is involved and benefiting from it. Women have helped men to grow. This is a human movement, and we need it plenty."

"What would happen if we lost the woman's movement?" I asked. "Oh, you can't go back," the older woman said and gasped at the thought.

"I'd still be in bed sleeping," the secretary said, "and I'd have more money."

"We'd regain a family-oriented society and have time for our children," the first student said. "Society would be a lot better off."

The other women in the room, except for the secretary whose head was nodding, turned and looked at her. There was a moment of total silence and then the student added, with a giggle and a sigh. "But I don't know. I'd be awful bored staying home. You can only shop so much, you know."

In one conversation I had heard it all: woman as powerful, woman as respected, woman as victim, woman as troublemaker, woman as mother, woman as ornament, woman as person, woman so sure she'd arrived at that point of humanity that is self-directing, autonomous, free, and valued that she doesn't even think of the woman's movement now. I knew instantly that the question was a central one and a complex one. The real truth lay surely in the fact that the woman's movement has both failed and succeeded and that sometimes it was hard to tell one dimension of it from the other.

What has the woman's movement really managed to do?

Part of the answer, of course, lies in determining where you want to start with the answer, at the suffragettes or at the publication of Betty Friedan's *The Feminine Mystique*. If we start with the suffragettes, of course, it is clear that we now have a female electorate in what had otherwise been a male republic for the 150 years prior to my grandmother's time.

If we start with Betty Friedan, on the other hand, we have a situation that may be more amazing perhaps than the gaining of the right to vote itself. Now we also have a female electorate that is strong enough and clear enough to be courted by politicians and analyzed by exit polls. There is a recognized woman's agenda and women candidates for public office and a woman's caucus in the Congress of the United States that monitors and promotes and writes and presses for legislation that is favorable to the concerns of women. In a culture historically more attuned to the problems of General Motors or the Pentagon or the savings and loan institutions of the country, it is no small thing to have someone notice legislation that discriminates against women or, worse perhaps, simply ignores the issues of child care or food stamps or medical assistance because the children, the poor, the elderly women of the world have no voice, no organization, no time for protest while they struggle in the lowest of low-paying jobs to support the children of the men who abandoned or beat them.

The women's movement has forced academia to admit male and female students on equal terms rather than on the quota systems of the 1970s that required higher admissions criteria of young women than young men for far fewer available places. Girls have the right to full physical development programs now. They can compete in intercollegiate sports and have fully salaried coaches and team busses. But they don't, for the most part, get prime-time television coverage. And they don't get high-paying professional salaries no matter how good they are. Worse, we know that it isn't the idea of women working that is the problem. Women are definitely allowed to work the food stands at men's games for slave wages or cheerlead in scanty clothes for absolutely no pay at all. But most women's sports still have not become as respected and common as men's. The continuing question, of course, has to be, Why?

We have to ask why women are denied constitutional rights and education and property and freedom throughout the world, and we must look to our theological concepts of God and creation and men for the answer.

We must ask why women work many more hours than men do in this country alone and ask what our churches teach about the role of women for an answer.

We must ask why women are paid significantly less than men for work that is every bit as difficult, every bit as important, and face what our churches maintain is the will of God for half the human race to understand the social situation.

The woman's movement has done much in society but most important of all, perhaps, the woman's movement has brought the theology of the church to a point of new development without which social structures will never change.

John XXIII in the encyclical "Pacem in Terris" called the shifting role of women one of "the signs of the times" along with the emergence of the Third World and the plight of the poor. And, good Pope John also writes in that document, that "those who discover that they have rights have the responsibility to claim them."

It is the claiming of those rights in the image of God, it is the development of a theology of humanity that will determine either the success or failure of the woman's movement. It may at the same time determine the future of the church as well.

Another old tale is important, I think, to our own understanding of how meaningful the woman's movement is to the spiritual life of us all. This story tells that once upon a time a Holy One who lived as a hermit on the mountain was asked by a disciple, "Holy One, what is the Way?"

"What a fine mountain this is," the Holy One said in reply. "I am not asking you about the mountain," the disciple said, "I am asking you about the Way."

And the Holy One replied, "So long as you cannot go beyond the mountain, my friend, you cannot reach the Way."

The woman's movement raises the most important questions of life. It forces us to face and think about and deal with the nature of relationships, the nature of humanity, and the nature of God. There can be no real holiness without it.

The implications are clear: If we do not go beyond this mountain, we cannot reach the Way.

It is time to realize that because we have not seen women as persons, full of grace, made in the image of God, that we have a world governed by one-half of the human heart, understood by only one-half of the human mind, and grown to only half the stature of the human soul. We are a handicapped people and a handicapped church.

We have done quite well considering our affliction, but we are not well, we are not whole, we are not totally human yet.

Indeed, we too have loved Eshun secretly but we have failed to embrace her in public. And it shows. In both church and state.

Clearly we are missing the mountain.

# Ministry

At this moment in history, ministry must differ from mere professional service. At this moment in history if our ministry is indeed to be real and effective and gospel and true, it needs to be a ministry to a wounded world.

Two stories show us the way. The first story comes from the Sufi. "Once upon a time," the story goes, "a seeker went from land to land to discover an authentic religion. Finally the seeker found a group of extraordinary fame: They were known for the goodness of their lives and for the singleness of their hearts and for the sincerity of their service. 'I see all of that,' the seeker said, 'and I'm impressed by it. But, before I become your disciple, I have a question to ask: Does your God work miracles?' And the disciple said, 'Well, it all depends on what you mean by a miracle. Some people call it a miracle when God does the will of people. We call it a miracle when people do the will of God.'" Ministry is as much, it seems, about bringing the reign of God as it is about doing good.

The wisdom of the ancients is as clear and as valid as ever: if we want to minister to the wounded in this world, if we really

want to do something important in this world, something meaningful in this life, we are going to have to concentrate on valuing
life before death and on working a few miracles of our own. Jobs
are easy to come by; careers are simple to fashion. There are bu-
reaucratic services aplenty, but what we really need are ministers.

The question is: where shall we go to determine how to minister to the marginalized minorities, the disinterested parish-
ioner, the alienated prisoner, the depressed elderly, the invisible
woman, the abandoned gay and lesbian, the displaced worker, the
desperate refugee, the neglected child, that is beyond the good
word, the warm smile, the caring call, the ministerial glad hand?

What can we do in our time that exceeds the "go-well-stay-
warm-and-well-fed" mentality that scripture warns about in the
letter of James (2:16) and that the wounded have learned to ignore? How shall we minister, in other words, in ways that change
people's lives as much as they warm their environment? How shall
we minister, too, in ways that change our own lives in this vast
and deadening world from the ranks of the burned-out humdrum
to the steady, steady godliness of the gospel?

That answer might be found in the second story, this one from
Christian scriptures, that is often translated as a glimpse of glory,
or worse, a case for contemplative withdrawal from the chaos
around us but which I believe is really an insight into the spirituality of dailiness, a call to courage, and a model for the kind of
ministry that changes things for the poor and marginal rather
than maintains them. It is the story of the Transfiguration. The
story of the Transfiguration is a journey into ministry with all
its misconceptions and all its misunderstandings and all its mis-
takes and all its mighty power.

Mount Tabor, the site of the Transfiguration, is one of those
places that is not "on the way" to anywhere. Mount Tabor is
steep and rugged and hard to scale.

The path that leads to the top of the mountain is hand-hewn
out of rock. It is also narrow and dangerous and long. Then, at
the top, with the exception of the view of the vast unending plain
of Jezreel below, there is nothing there. It's an out-of-the-way

place that has all the character of a dead-end—a beautiful dead-end, true, but a dead-end nevertheless. And it is Tabor to which Jesus took Peter, James, and John. If we want to understand precisely what ministry is really all about, all we have to do is look at Peter, James, and John on Tabor!

In the first place, Peter, James, and John thought they had been called to go up the mountain to be with Jesus alone. So, the scripture says, "they 'left the world' below and went off by themselves," prepared, apparently, to follow Jesus and find God.

Mountains in ancient spiritualities, Judaism included, were always points of contact with God because they were the places where earth touched heaven. To go "up to a high mountain" —to which there are eight major references in the Judeo-Christian scriptures—is always then to be seeking a very special relationship with God.

On this particular excursion up this particular mountain, theirs was a very select group: no one else was with them and they did indeed have Jesus all to themselves. And, sure enough, scripture records that a strange and wonderful thing occurred there.

Up on the top of that faraway mountain Peter, James, and John got a new insight into Jesus. Up there, by themselves, they began to see Jesus differently. And he was a great deal more than they had ever even imagined: he was as dazzling as the sun—he was as intense, and he was all-consumed as well as all-consuming. The idea was overwhelming. And very, very heady. It was also very, very disturbing.

Because then and there, in a gospel that is apparently about the mystical, the privatized, dimension of life with Jesus, we begin to see the perennial struggle between piety and Christianity, between comfort and compassion, between social service and godly ministry, between the barely therapeutic and the deeply healing, between religion-for-real and religion-for-show. There, on the top of the mountain, right in front of their eyes, Jesus, the scripture says, became transfigured before them, radiant as the sun and talking to Moses and Elijah . . . to Moses and Elijah!

And there's the part of the story that makes the difference—

the real difference—to our ministry. Why? If we are going to see ministry to the wounded as our own task at this time in history, then it's important to realize four things about this gospel:

#1    In the first place, Peter himself opted for piety. "Jesus, it's good for us to be here," Peter said. After all, Peter knows a good thing when he sees it. And Peter plans to settle down here and now. "Let's build three booths. . . ."

At the very moment of his deepest revelation and his clearest call, Peter decides that the spiritual life has something to do with building temples and enlarging the office and saying proper prayers or praying properly and floating above the fray. After all, the company is choice, the office is comfortable, and the environment is nothing if not rarified.

Indeed, if there is a temptation in Christian ministry it is probably the temptation to play church, to dabble in religion, to recite the creed without feeling any moral compulsion whatsoever to render it in flesh and blood. And therein lies the second signifi-

#2    cant dimension of the story, the almost cacophonous cry of this scripture: no sooner has Peter decided to be a church bureaucrat, a weekday mystic, an office manager than look what happens: Scripture dashes the entire thought in midair. "While he was still speaking," the scripture records, "the voice of God says, 'This is my son. . . . Listen!'" And then, the passage continues, Jesus laid his hands on them and said, very simply, very directly: "Get up. And do not be afraid."

#3    Then, in the third scene of the story, slowly but surely, Jesus began to lead them around the edges of the cliffs, over the rocky road, back down the mountain to the very bottom of the hill: to the dirty towns and hurting people and unbelieving officials and ineffective institutions below where the sick and outcast, the abandoned and infected waited for them expecting to be healed. And they had every right to expect it—because Jesus didn't appear to Peter, James, and John with David, the king, or with Aaron, the priest.

Jesus didn't show himself to the disciples with those who interpreted the law or defined the worship of the society—Jesus didn't reveal his work as either royalty or ritual. No! Jesus identified himself on Tabor with Moses and Elijah. With Moses who had led people out of oppression, and with Elijah whom King Ahab called "that troubler of Israel," the one who condemned the compromise between true and false gods; the one, in other words, who exposed to the people the underlying causes of their problems.

Jesus, the minister, identified himself not with the kings and the priests of Israel who had maintained its establishments and developed its institutions, good as they were; no, Jesus, the healer, identified himself with the prophets, with those who had been sent to warn Israel of its unconscionable abandonment of the covenant. Surely there isn't a minister alive today who doesn't understand the pain and the power of this gospel. Because this gospel is the very bedrock lesson of ministry: if ministry is to have any meaning whatsoever in our times, then every minister, too, will have to wade into the throngs of hurting people on every plain of this planet, listening, listening, listening to the prophet-healer Jesus and exposing to people the underlying causes of all the wounding in this world. And all of that in the face of those institution-types for whom saving the system is much too often a higher priority than saving the people.

Of course, the call to Christian ministry presupposes a long, long journey up a mountain to find God. But the call to ministry also means that we simply cannot build a spiritual life and expect to stay on the top of our pious and antiseptic little mountains. The call of the spiritual life, then, the call of ministry, is the call to take all the insights into the life of Christ that we have ever been able to gather down from our private little mountains to the grasping, groaning world of our own time. The call to ministry today is the call to be aware of the root causes of suffering in this world and to work a few miracles of our own.

We work with poor women and battered women and undernourished women every day—and we do that very well. But how can we possibly say that we really minister to women and do nothing, say nothing, about the fact that women get paid 25 to 33 percent less than men for the very same work, or that, with all of the myths about "progress," of the 500 CEOs of the *Fortune* 500 companies only a handful are women; and of their over 2,000 corporate officers not even 100 are women because women seldom get promoted to top management positions.

How can we say that we minister to women and say nothing about the fact that a married man can be an ordained deacon but a married woman cannot, despite fourteen centuries of tradition of women deaconesses to counter whatever theological, historical, and biological arguments might be raised! How can we possibly minister to women and agree that God can be called rock, tree, key, wind, door, and dove in centuries of litanies without bringing the church to perdition, but we can never, ever call the God who is endless being, eternal womb, mother.

How can we think we minister to women and erase them from the very pronouns of the church; and how can we tell them that they may not even think that the God who made them, too, "in God's own image" might have outrageous plans for them in the economy of salvation. How can we ignore these things and think that change will come for women until we advocate for change in both state and church?

We minister to the hungry and the unemployed and the depressed every day—and we do that very well. But how can we say that we really minister to the poor if we never so much as question the fact that in this country we are still putting more money into weapons of destruction, and still waging election campaigns based on that, than we are putting into works of human development?

How can we possibly say that we're doing enough to minister to the homeless and the poor and the uneducated and the ill and the emotionally broken, and never do a thing, never say a thing to reform a military economy that consumes more of our resources than that allotted for military use by any other nation in the world, and is, at the same time, eroding our social system and numbing our consciences and consuming our scientists and eating out the very heart of the country with its bias for violence?

We minister to hurting families by listening, and caring, and planning—and we do all of that very well. But how can we see families on the verge of collapse because their finances are on the verge of collapse and never say a word about the imbalance of our national budget or the loss of our industries to Global South laborers reduced to industrial slavery, or the tragedy of the six million working poor in this country who work two jobs for less than one full-time salary, or work full-time for part-time pay and no benefits, and think we're doing all we can for the hurting families we see? How can we say that we are really ministering to poor families and never say a word about welfare for the rich which we call "tax breaks" and "corporate incentives" while people dare to criticize welfare for the poor that we call food stamps and universal medical insurance?

We minister with warmth and care to the drug addicts and the deprived and the illiterate who wind up in our prisons—and we do that very well. But how can we say we're ministering to prisoners and do nothing to promote the rehabilitation of the prison system itself while prisons are the one growth industry in many parts of a country whose schools are deteriorating? How can we say that we're concerned about prisoners and do nothing to reverse the scourge of a capital punishment that we now know, given the advent of DNA testing, is averaging one innocent death for every seven executions?

We minister to the traumatized and the homesick and the frightened in our armed forces with affection and presence and parental concern—and we do that very well. But how can we minister to men and women in the armed forces—tell them that we care about them and that love is the only Christian imperative—and never ourselves say a thing about the immorality of nuclear war or preemptive war or biological war or the nuclear policies and the nuclear mentalities that make nuclearism possible? How can we lay the morality of nuclearism and the burden of conscientious objection and the preservation of the planet on the consciences of nineteen-year-olds who are not old enough to buy a bottle of beer in thirty-seven states of the union?

We minister to the angry and the depressed and the

despairing with consistency and Christian hope—and we do that very well. But how can we call ourselves ministers and never speak out about the lack of gun control laws in a country in which the blood of our own children runs in our streets because as a country we have taught them violence very well?

We stand for life and human development by being with people in pain—and we do that very well. But how can we cry and cry and cry about abortion—as important, as imperative as that issue is—as if it were a single-issue subject, but say nothing about the parental role of men or the equality of women or the lack of day care programs or the loss of subsidized housing or the absence of food programs for children or the planned destruction of the planet that wrings life out of people after birth an inch at a time? And who of us will have ministered to that? And in whom of us will those at the bottom of the mountain see a different transfiguration story?

The transfiguration is about more than what happens on the mountain, though go to the mountain every minister must, if only to see for ourselves and to become what we can become and to get a view of the people on the plain below through the eyes of Moses and Elijah and Jesus.

Service, people can pay for and many people do. But ministry, real ministry, is priceless, and can be done only in the name of Jesus, not in the name of careers, professions, or promotions. Service is a teachable skill. Ministry is the mark of Elijah who resisted the government to reveal the true God, and of Moses who resisted the people to reveal the law of God, and of Jesus the healing prophet, the prophet-healer who demanded more from the disciples than personal faith alone. Jesus demanded commitment to the bringing of the reign of God, here, now.

Indeed, the problem with the story of the Transfiguration is that it has two parts—first there is the top of the mountain, but the second part, in the same chapter, in run-on lines, takes place on the plain below. And it is this second part that is for us, as it was for the apostles, the real measure of ministry.

When Jesus and the disciples came down from the Mount of

the Transfiguration, suffering people in droves were waiting for Jesus below. And the scripture is quite clear why. "I have brought my son to you because he is possessed by a demon. . . . I asked your disciples to expel him, but they were unable to do so." And the disciples, scripture says, began to ask Jesus privately, "Why is it that we could not expel the demon?" And Jesus told them, "This kind is driven out only by prayer."

This kind is driven out only by insight, by vision, by contemplation and the compassion that comes from it, not simply by technique, not by organizational niceties and canon law and clericalism. This kind is driven out only by prayer—by "putting on the mind of Christ," not by putting on more titles or roles or uniforms or offices or money. This kind is driven out only by soul-sightedness, only by risk, only by courage, only by a care that supersedes cost, only by a heart devoted to causes rather than to symptoms. This kind is driven out only by the spirit of Moses and Elijah, whom kings expelled and professionals despised and the temple feared, but to whom the people looked for truth.

And that's today's problem, and this moment's challenge to ministry: here at the bottom of the mountain people look to us now, to be the vision, to bring the truth, to expel the demons.

We live in an information culture today. The World Wide Web grows by seventeen pages per second, and the world has generated more data in the last thirty years than it did in the preceding five hundred. And change is as rapid as the communications system that transmits it. The question is: who will evaluate the changes and critique the consequences of each on the human spirit, if not those who minister to the spirits that are being broken by them?

We live in a high-tech culture which needs desperately to compensate for the impersonalism of technology by the rediscovery of human values. The question is: who will call a world on the brink of death by technological self-destruction to the cry of human community if not you and I?

We live in a culture where industry is fast moving both its high-tech jobs as well as its sweatshops but not its medical insurance or pension plans or Fair Labor Standards Act to the Global South today. The question is: who will call for building bridges across our cultural differences instead of building fences around our borders, so that by developing others we also develop ourselves?

We live in a world where short-term advantage must give way to long-term planning and concern for consequences, before pollution and quarterly profit and international debt make the people of the planet an afterthought. The United States has forgiven the bilateral debt of the most highly indebted countries and could easily forgive the bilateral debt of middle-income debtor countries with a fraction of what it hopes to spend on a nuclear shield. The question is: who will call the world to care about the afterwards of profit, pollution, and international debt if not those of us who are already ministering to the displaced and dispossessed?

Participation has become the order of the day. Every group and people and place, no matter their size—Kurds, Tutsis, East Timorese, and women—want to be a part of the process of arriving at decisions that affect their lives. The question is: who will help people in this situation to help themselves if not those who say that their goal is to minister to the needy, not simply to maintain them?

We live in a world where information is toppling the old pyramids of inherited power. Institutions and hierarchies have failed to solve society's problems, and people are beginning to rise up together—in the woman's movement and the peace movement, and the ethnic identity movement, and the save-the-whales movement—to do it themselves. The question is: who will help the people at the foot of the mountain to turn the transfiguring light of Christ into the dark spots of life where the suffering wait for the demons to be expelled if not those who, this time, minister day and night, night and day, to those made helpless by those systems?

We live in a world with a shifting economic center that is leaving in its wake a whole new world of poverty and unemployment and undersubsidized public services that breed crime and destitution and ignorance and malnutrition and underdevelopment and revolutionary anger. And new improved political meanness to control it. The question is: who will care for the people left behind? Who will set out to reform the system if not those who minister firsthand to the results of the damage it wreaks?

We are ministering in parishes well, but now we must transform the parishes from islands of ritual to arenas of prophetic participation. We are ministering in prisons well, but now we must transform the prisons from places of punishment to centers of newfound dignity.

We are ministering to neglected women well, but now we must enable women to gain the fullness of humanity, the center of the gospel life, not simply a hard-won, long-suffering faith.

We are ministering at bedsides well, but now we must bring the ill and the dying a hope of their importance in our national agenda and attention to the cost of their care, not simply the warmth of our presence.

We must be for the poor not simply a handout but a voice on their behalf where the poor are not heard and their pain is not registered. If we are really to minister, it is up to us to first be transformed ourselves so that we can then be really transfiguring. We must be aware not simply of the pain but of why the hurting hurts. And then we must set out not simply to comfort or care for them but to do something to cure the causes as well as the symptoms.

Those are things of which we must be aware if we are to be authentic. And, if we are truly to minister to a wounded world, those are the miracles that we must now begin to work. And when others say that's not our role, we must remember that Jesus appeared with Elijah, the troublemaker, and Moses, the liberator. And when we're tempted to think that we're already too busy doing so much good where we are to do anything more, we must remember Jesus wading into the crowd below.

To be a minister at this moment, we must do a charity based on justice, we must give a charity that seeks justice.

It is not charity, it is not love, to bind up wounds made by the system but to do nothing to change the system that is doing the wounding. Our ministry is to continue the work not only of Jesus the Healer but also of Jesus the Prophet. Our ministry must be not only to comfort but to challenge state, community, and church—not just to attend to the pain but to advocate for change; to be not just a vision but a voice; not simply to care for the victims of the world but also to change the institutions that victimize them. "If we had been holier people," the essayist Templeton teaches us, "we would have been angrier oftener."

The desert monastics tell the story of ministry this way: past a seeker on a prayer rug came the cripples and the beggars and the beaten. And seeing them, the seeker went down, down, down into deep prayer and cried: "Great God! If you are a great God, how is it that a loving creator can see such things and do nothing about them?" And out of the long, long silence, the voice of God came back: "I did do something about them. I made you."

What does it mean to minister today, early on in a new century, a new mountaintop, a new millennium, a new moment in history? It means awareness, authenticity, and transfiguration. Transfiguration for us all—for the sake of their souls, of course, but for the sake of our own souls as well.

# Vision

〜

Is the call of Vatican II still current? Framing these reflections is a story from the Book of Kings: "... in those days God called Samuel. . . ." But Samuel did not as yet recognize the voice of God. "Visions," scripture says, "were scarce in those days," and so Samuel went instead to the priest of the temple, saying, "Eli, you called me. Here I am." But Eli said, "I did not call you. Go back to sleep." Finally after Samuel was called three times, Eli, of whom scripture says, "Eli's eyes were growing dim," instructed Samuel to say, "Lord, here I am." And Samuel did, and what the Lord told Samuel was that Eli's days as high priest were over because there were elements in the old system that had to be changed, things his sons did which Eli had not corrected. What can we possibly think about such a serious situation as this? What can we possibly learn from it in our own time?

First, we must remember that Eli was going blind. Eli was no longer able to see what needed to be done next. But one thing you can say for Eli: Eli, the institution itself, enabled Samuel, taught Samuel, ordered Samuel to hear beyond the institution to the voice of God in his life. And more than that. We must realize that the

voice of God to Samuel was that the very institution that had
formed him was to be re-formed by him. What Eli had taught him
he was to use to correct Eli's world. No doubt about it: Samuel is
the saint of Vatican II.

Bella Lewitzky, woman of a wandering people, once wrote,
"To move freely you must be deeply rooted." Without doubt, roots
and wings are of a piece. One without the other is bogus. To renew the church we must be faithful to the church, and to renew
the church we must stretch the church. The question is simply,
Stretch it to what? And how?

In what way is the call of Vatican II still current? Is religion
itself really of urgent value in today's world? Is organized religion worth the struggle? At its best, religion offers more than a
list of answers. Like Eli, it tenders a way to deal with the questions that plague our lives. This transition from certainty to faith,
from faithful answers to faithful questions is a slow one. It is the
transition from roots to wings. It is the difference between Call to
Action 1976 and Call to Action today.

Call to Action 1976 was an attempt to make real what was
clearly present in the then fresh documents of Vatican II. Call to
Action today is a call to make present what is not so clearly evi-
dent in the now old documents of Vatican II but is still implied in
them, and must still be alive in us if we are to remain as committed to development as we are faithful to our roots. As committed
to our roots as we are faithful to development.

Thanks to Vatican II, ideas changed, and that frightened some
people. It cast others adrift, plunged many into blind resistance.
But it energized the rise of another whole church for whom the
past was the glue needed to reconfigure a healthier future.
Essence remained: 1. God is. 2. Openness to the world is the way
of Jesus, and 3. the Holy Spirit lives in each of us. Those are the
givens, the things that do not change. Those are the roots that
give us wings. In fact, on those ideas has rested the unity of the
church and the development of the faith for centuries as the world
tilted and turned.

And the world around us, like the world after Galileo and the world after the Enlightenment and the world after the fall of the monarchies in Europe, is shifting like a glacier in sunlight. Now, in our time, we have again a culture in flux and questions in embryo, and gods in conflict, and tensions—personal, social, local, global, international, organizational—aplenty. The question is not whether the faith is believable. The real question is whether that faith is meaningful to us, here and now. We live in a desert between two places: one at the brink of Vatican II, just over the edge of Vatican I, a relatively static world where change and doubt were little tolerated. The other, this world, a borderless world exploding with information, bristling with independence, inundated with questions, teeming with the agitation and the rage of the oppressed and invisible.

The world races blindly by us unsure what, if anything, religion has to offer a wounded, worried, weary world that is awash in clonings and stem cell research, comic book star-wars weapons and the desperate poverty that militarism and nuclear holocaust breed—and now fear, great fear, and houses divided against themselves with a microcosm of world religions in every major city in the world. The world is now a place that prays in many languages at one time.

What are we to be about in church renewal if the church itself is to keep pace? Today's questions for Call to Action must be: Why must the church be in the world? How must the church be in the world? And what must the church do now to really be a leavening presence in such a world?

The situation is fraught with danger. It seems we are being asked to ignore the obvious and abandon the vision of Vatican II. On the other hand, we find ourselves without the moorings of the soul it takes to stay a course in dark times, to trust that the Holy Spirit is working in this confusion. But such a situation is not a new one.

In ancient times, when Greek mythology ceased to satisfy the new commitment to the orderly, rational pursuit of evidence, philosophers then, too, began to point out the contradictions inherent in popular theology. Who was really God if there were many gods?

What kind of religion was it that dealt with humanity in some kind of brutal sport? What was heaven if competition between the gods was par for the course, and chaos part and parcel of godliness there? The old myths condemned themselves by their own hand. Intelligent people began to feel distant from a system that was arbitrary and incongruent, destructive and unyielding. Religion reeled from the assault. Philosophy emerged with more reasonable answers to the problems of life than did religion.

Religion as the ancient Greeks had known it was dead. But which was the greater errancy, the mythological explanations of life given by religion or the rational imaginings of the new purveyors of philosophical ideas? In fact, which is the greater errancy today, the distance from the world of a clerical church under siege before Vatican II, or the wildly committed imaginings of the "people of God" after it?

The answer lies now, I think, as it did then, in the relationship between roots and wings, between respect for the past and commitment to the present. Social turbulence is always a sure sign that the faith must be rethought, reinterpreted, restated in the light of present circumstances. It is not the first time in Catholic history that new spiritual understandings have emerged in the light of new questions, and new questions in the light of new understandings. The Council of Nicaea in 325, the Council of Constantinople in 381, the Athanasian Creed in the sixth century, even Pope Paul VI's "Credo of the People of God," published as late as 1968, all attempted, in the face of different questions, to reformulate the fundamentals in ways that could be understood by people at that time.

To question is not to deny. It may, in fact, be the truest type of faith, the most faithful kind of religion. If we are really to be faithful, to be rooted, we must ask ourselves again and again: What did Vatican II really mandate? Those are our roots. And what is left to be done? Those are the things that must give us wings.

Against what must we struggle? And from what can we draw hope? The answer lies in looking again at the *Documents of Vatican II*, with both their turning points and tensions.

1. In the *Dogmatic Constitution on the Church*, the turning point is the very definition of the church itself. In Baltimore Catechism days, the definition was structural and very straightforward. "The church," every child learned, "was that body of lawfully baptized faithful who accepted the teachings of the church, were gathered around the local bishop who was in communion with the church in Rome."

Vatican II enlarged that definition of church, gave us new roots. The church, the council declared, is "the people of God." There and then the focus shifts beyond the hierarchical, beyond spiritual childhood, beyond being consumers of faith to being carriers of faith. But then the tensions multiply too. The whole question of role definitions—of who does what, of gifts and responsibilities, of who's in charge of what, of relationships and ecclesiology, of who is more important than whom in the church—become new points of theological departure.

People who do not "belong" to a church but who "are" the church begin to take that focus seriously and in ways that alter past patterns and beliefs. They begin to make clear that they want their church open to women, open to homosexuals, open to married priests, open to women priests and preachers, open to lay consultation. In other words, they want their wings.

2. In the *Dogmatic Constitution on Divine Revelation* the place of scripture in Catholic formation re-energized literary exegesis and historical scholarship, areas dormant in Roman circles for eons. This fresh encouragement of biblical study raises new issues as well. Whether or not revelation is ongoing may become even more problematic now. Consequently, an understanding of "tradition" that is based on historical patterns of practice and custom is now being contested in favor of new insights with firm scriptural foundation. If scripture, for instance, has nothing at all to say about the ordination of women, on what basis do we use Jesus as our right to obstruct it? It is the question of the place of scripture, the model of Jesus, in the development of doctrine that must give us all new wings.

3. The turning point in the *Constitution on the Sacred Liturgy,*

with its institution of the vernacular as an "official" language of consecration, was its concern to return the liturgy of the church to the people, who are the church. Gone was the notion that Eucharist was something done for us and on us instead of with us, something for a single priest in a dark crypt to "get in." It was all a great breakthrough for Christian community. But tensions lurk in these shadows, too. Uniformity, that long-heralded counterpoint of Catholic unity, became a point of contention about the nature of tradition.

When the bishops called the first Call to Action conference in 1976, I sat on the smallest committee, the committee on language. I told the committee that ours was the most volatile topic.

"Impossible," they told me. But the office of women's concerns, altar girls, theological study—these passed. Ours didn't. Our request for two tiny words to designate the whole human race didn't pass. The liturgy became a battleground where bread recipes, the gender, dress, and geography of altar servers and ministers became theologically central, and the translations of pronouns were centers of conflict and control. Mystique has again become confused with mystery. If we do not get beyond this, there will be no Eucharistic wings on which to fly.

4. In the *Pastoral Constitution on the Church in the Modern World,* the church in Vatican II turned squarely from an insular perspective which emphasized the separateness of the sacred and the secular, to the consideration of the integrity, the essential connectedness of the sacred and the secular. It was a transfiguring moment, never more than now. From a posture of resistance and rejection of the larger world, the church turned to a commitment to human advancement, to the development of world community, to the acceptance of science, and to a new concern for the economic and cultural development of all peoples as well as for their spiritual salvation. The transformation of society, in other words, is publicly declared in this key document as an essential part of the church's mission to humanity.

And so the tensions are clear. Someone must still ask, How

much involvement is too much involvement of church in the political system and political issues? When does advocacy become control? And when we argue for moral principles in the marketplace, whose morality shall it be and who decides? And how? By endorsing candidates, by forbidding the support of a candidate to people, to adults, to citizens of conscience—or by teaching principles? The answers are slow in coming but on them lies the very existence of wings.

5. The *Decree on Ecumenism* recognized officially the scandal of Christian division. What is more, this statement asserts a unity in vision and essential commitment among the whole Christian family. Finally, the paper affirms the diversity of gifts—liturgical, spiritual, and theological—that make up the whole church of Christ in all its denominations. But the challenge is to move Christian ecumenism beyond ecclesiastical get-togethers to the recognition of the single mission and the common table of the total Christian church. The scandal of division is not the scandal of the people. It is the scandal of professional church makers, and it must be repented before we can teach peace to anyone else. Indifferentism is not ecumenism, of course, but absolutism, on the other hand, erodes the witness of the full Christian presence, even when it comes packaged in documents from Rome. Conversion and repentance are imperatives of the church as well as its members.

Whatever recent documents, written again without the approbation of the church universal, say to the contrary about the salvific value of our sister churches, Vatican II and its outreach to the entire Christian dispensation is the root that gives the faith wings.

6. In the *Decree on the Bishops' Pastoral Office in the Church*, the church makes a screeching turn from medieval hierarchy to modern pastor. The bishop is not defined in these documents as "lord and lawgiver." His role is to enable the church, to be in touch with issues and ideas, to create a national identity. Clearly the question of international control of the newly heightened local church is the high water to be negotiated now. Without resolving this, pas-

toral paralysis will surely set in, ecclesiastical climbing for official favor will surely take over as bishops defer to Roman control rather than stand for national needs, until, in the end, bishops become unnecessary at all. To fly in the face, for instance, of national conferences of bishops and their authorization of liturgical translations for their own countries, let alone attempt to stop the renovation of a cathedral in midair, is not only to obviate the local church but to turn bishops into altar boys as well. It is to tie the wings we have been given.

7. The Vatican II *Decree on the Ministry and Life of Priests* and the *Decree on Priestly Formation* may someday be seen as pivotal to the development of the new church to which the earlier documents point. In these documents clericalism dies an official death, however prevalent it may still be. What is asked of the priest is, of course, the ability to form community, to lead the search for God but to acknowledge, to listen to, and to trust the laity whose gifts, the same documents say, are essential to the church. As the telling phrase of the documents, "Brother among brothers" [*sic*], celebrates, the priest is to be spiritual catalyst, not parish potentate. But the role revision sounds a great deal easier in theory than it is in practice. "Father says" is no longer enough to qualify for the running of a school, a ministry, or a parish unilaterally. From a position of "father," the patriarchal lawgiver of a Roman family in whose hands lie the life or death of the entire clan, the priest is now asked to assume the role of "brother," the documents say, of caring peer, of loving equal—even to the married and to women.

8. The *Decree on the Appropriate Renewal of Religious Life* came over four hundred years after the Council of Trent thought it had cast religious life in stone by declaring solemnly that it was just right as it was, wimples, walls, and all. No more ministries to consider, no more forms to create, no new orders to allow, no new rules to permit beyond those of the early orders—and then the Council called Vatican II called religious life to renew itself. More importantly, perhaps, the Council instructed religious to turn to the gospels, the initiating intent of their founders and the social realities of the times, not to church law or episcopal control, for

their criteria and direction. And these are dangerous directions all. The tensions surfaced almost immediately and are with us still. The dualistic notion that the essence of religious perfection lies in separation from the world and blind, military obedience lingers pathologically in the minds of a generation formed on false or symbolic asceticisms rather than on the searing demands of a gospel that cures lepers, raises women from the dead, and contends with Scribes and Pharisees from the temple to the tomb.

Transcending the world, then, becomes a counterweight to transforming it. So the renewal of religious life becomes a struggle to balance the claims of law against the touchstone of an experience rife with new poor, alive with new questions, challenged by new kinds of spirituality and spiritual adults. As a result, of the ministries listed in the Kennedy Directory, the registry of official Catholic organizations, over 75 percent were founded by religious communities while they were being called into chanceries and scolded for leaving the schools and not wearing religious uniforms.

Finally the question of whether or not religious life is to be fundamentally charismatic or functionally institutional simmers at the center of the renewal of religious life. Whether religious are to animate or simply to staff the works they undertake in a church in whom all are called to minister and lead and teach and serve remains a determining issue. Are women religious to be the good sisters, the darling daughters of the church, or the dangerous women sent from the tomb with a message on their minds and a gospel in their hands? The struggle between control and charism is getting stronger every day as religious use their roots to justify their wings.

9. That the role of the laity in the church was even an issue at Vatican II may be the greatest turning point of the church's modern history. In the *Decree on the Apostolate of the Laity* the lay state in the church began, for the first time in history, to be described as a "vocation." The laity were instructed in this document that the believer "has both a right and a duty to use their gifts" in the church. Participation rather than passivity became a factor of lay commitment. From that rationale came the call to the laity to be

responsible for church organization, for Catholic education, for religious formation programs, for church administration and for thoughtful, considered reflection, for the *sensus fidelium* that John Henry Newman gifted to the modern church.

The inherent tension in this development of the laity is at least twofold. This departure from clericalism raises the issue of authority. When competency lies with the lay leader, to what degree is the priest in charge of parish or school, and why? Second, if the laity really are gifted for the sake of the Christian community, does this mean lay women, too, or only lay men? And if it does mean women, why are they not being generally, wholly, totally accepted in worship or administration, in the diaconate, at least, for which we have centuries of women deacons as models? Here history, theology, and law all come together to confront and expose the debilitating sexism of the church. If I were a Roman Catholic bishop in this country, I would not be disturbed that Catholic women were throwing themselves on the steps of the cathedrals begging to minister in the church. I would be disturbed that they had to go to Protestant seminaries for the theological and pastoral preparation to do it.

If Roman Catholic dioceses continue to refuse to prepare women for participation in the church, I predict that this movement of Catholic women to Protestant schools of theology will significantly alter the shape of the church, the faith, in the next 25 years. The preparation of the laity guarantees that the church will always have the wings it needs.

10. In the *Decree on the Church's Missionary Activity,* the turning point is attitudinally so deep that perhaps only a Catholic can sense its real depth. Two new postures are affirmed here. The first is that conversion must be free. With this statement hundreds of years of church-state control are abandoned by a church whose entire middle history was embedded in theocratic governments. The second notion is that missionaries are to be more presence than proselytizers. They are to become inculturated, and, as quickly as possible, enable the new church to become a native

church. According to the document, at least, Western ecclesiastical imperialism is finally over.

However, this growing shift in the center of the church from First to Third World peoples in population, character, and tone has done little or nothing to dislodge Roman curial control. Tension is inherent here. How long new native churches will tolerate Western formulations, Western interpretations, Western liturgical forms, and Western theological analysis is anybody's guess. The Chinese church, in fact the entire Asian church, and that other newly recognized mission church—the American one—are growing wings.

11. The *Declaration on the Relationship of the Church to Non-Christian Religions* is a time bomb waiting to go off. In a dramatic move, this declaration from a council of the church, solemnly assembled, asserts that as Christians we must accept "all that is true and holy" in non-Christian religions. Imagine! We are clearly saying that in Buddhism, in Hinduism, in Judaism, in Islam there is something "true and holy." After centuries of their repudiation, moreover, the church officially condemns in this statement any persecution or discrimination based on race, color, condition of life, or religion. The implications for world development and the creation of human community are far-ranging but late and incomplete: late for Tissa Balasuriya and his call to watch the language of original sin in cultures that see original perfection, late for gays and lesbians who are yet to be seen more as normal than "disordered," late for women who are still considered outside the pale of a God who parts the seas, draws water from a rock, and raises the dead to life, but cannot and will not work through a woman. Apparently femaleness is the only substance before which God goes impotent.

More, no consciousness of the effects of pluralism in the new multicultural governments is found in this document. The issues of school prayer and the hanging of Judeo-Christian commandments in U.S. courtrooms as the basis for judicial norms, in a government based on the separation of church and state, both of which are now emerging with a vengeance, threaten the very pluralism which, as a nation, we espouse and as a global people we can no longer avoid. The tensions residual in both those realities are yet to be recognized as issues of faith but are, I submit, very real indicators of the presence or absence of true Christians. It is no longer learning to function as a Christian in a non-Christian world that is essential. It is learning to function as a Christian in a non-Christian neighborhood that is essential to the integrity of both state and church.

12. In the *Declaration on Religious Freedom* the revolutionary tenet is simply that conscience must be the primary determinant of religious conviction. Everyone, everyone—even nuns and priests, I assume—is immune from coercion in the name of religion.

The problem is clear: Someone, somewhere must come to grips with coercion. Is legislative pressure or church-state collusion to write denominational morality into law "coercion"? And, if it isn't, whose morality shall it be in a multicultural society in a world without borders? What is the line between church and state? What is the place for conscience in individuals and what does that have to do with the development of doctrine and the measure of our own Catholicity? Who does the measuring?

People do not question because they reject the church. They question the church because they love the church. They question because they seek a spiritual life, with or without an institution, and even outside of it, if being in it is what makes the spiritual life impossible for them. Most of all, they question because the church itself has created an ideal which too often it then does not itself seek. That is what happened to Martin Luther, and Catherine of Siena, and Dorothy Day, and Thomas Merton. They did not question because they did not believe what the church taught; they questioned because they did.

And that's what happened to you and me. They taught the unity-making dimensions of the Eucharist and we believed it. They taught the holy-making power of scripture and we believed it. They taught the community-making power of the church and we believed it. They taught equality and we believed it. In

Vatican II they taught a whole new way of being church—and we believed them.

Being rooted in Vatican II is not enough to make yourself a Vatican II Catholic. It is just as necessary to develop Vatican II as it is to preserve it, to grow its wings as to prune its branches. And each of these documents of Vatican II cries out yet for wings by believers who are as committed to the present and dedicated to the future as they are rooted in the past.

For the next 25 years it is not necessary to repeat the agenda of Vatican II, but to complete it. We are struggling now with silencings for thinkers and *mandatums* for theologians, and recipes for liturgy and a newly emerging authoritarian pastoring and a parallel priesthood independent of local bishops and more committed to some transcendent ideology than to the enculturation of the local church—a system to be reckoned with in the future.

But there are signs of great hope as well. There are lay theologians now who speak a bold truth. There are groups who know they are the new church in embryo: Dignity and the Association for the Rights of Catholics in the Church and Women's Ordination Conference. Quixote Center and Pax Christi and the Center of Concern and the Leadership Conference of Women Religious and Conference of Major Superiors of Men. And especially Call to Action, this great flowing movement of faithful hearts. There is, most of all, the Holy Spirit who refuses to give up on us. And finally there is Samuel, who allowed the institution to lead him to the voice of God and then built a new people in the shadows of the old. There are the wings that come from Vatican II itself to carry us—because of our roots—beyond our roots. The message of Vatican II at this moment is still: Go on! Fly, church, fly!

# Discipleship

⸻

*T*wo stories may explain these reflections on discipleship in an interim age best. The first insight is from the poet Basho who wrote: "I do not seek to follow in the footsteps of those of old. I seek the things they sought."

And the second story is from ancient monastic literature: Once upon a time, the story goes, a teacher traveled with great difficulty to a faraway monastery because there was an old monastic there who had a reputation for asking very piercing spiritual questions. "Holy One," the teacher said. "Give me a question that will renew my soul." "Ah, yes, then," the old monastic said, "your question is, What do they need?"

The teacher wrestled with the question for days but then, depressed, gave up and went back to the old monastic in disgust. "Holy One," the teacher said, "I came here because I'm tired and depressed and dry. I didn't come here to talk about my ministry. I came here to talk about my spiritual life. Please give me another question." "Ah, well, of course. Now I see," the old monastic said, "in that case, the right question for you is not, What do they need? The right question for you is, What do they really need?"

The question haunts me. What do the people really need in a period when the sacraments are being lost in a sacramental church but all approaches to the question—even the consciousness that there is a question to be asked conscientiously about the nature and meaning of priesthood—is being blocked, obstructed, denied, and suppressed?

"What do they really need?" becomes a haunting refrain in me for more reasons than the philosophical. Up at the top of a Mexican mountain, beyond miles of rutted road and wet, flowing clay, I toured an Indian village that was visited by a priest only once a year. But that was years ago. Now the mountain is just as high and the priest is fifteen years older.

Five years ago I spoke in an American parish of 6,000 families—one of those new Western phenomena known as "mega-churches" that is served by three priests. There is no priest shortage there, however, the priests want you to know, because the bishop has redefined the optimum ratio of priest to people from one to every 250 families to one priest to every 2,000 families. In diocese after diocese parishes are being merged, closed, turned into sacramental way stations served by retired priests or married male deacons, both of which are designed to keep the church male, whether it is ministering or not. The number of priests is declining. The number of Catholics is increasing, the number of lay ministers being certified is rising in every academic system despite the fact that their services are being restricted, rejected, or made redundant in parish after parish.

And in the United States, there's a five-year-old girl who, when her parents answered her question about the absence of women priests in their parish with the flat explanation that "We don't have girl-priests in our church," thought for a minute and then responded sharply, "Then why do we go there?"!

Clearly, the church is changing even while it reasserts its changelessness.

It is a far cry from the dynamism of the early church in which Prisca and Lydia and Thecla and Phoebe and hundreds of women like them opened house churches, walked as disciples of Paul, "constrained him," the scripture says, to serve a given region, instructed people in the faith and ministered to the fledgling Christian communities with no apology, no argument, no tricky theological shell games about whether they were ministering *in persona Christi* or *in nomine Christi.*

Clearly, both the question and the answer are clear: What do they really need? They need what they needed when the temple became more important than the Torah; they need what they needed when the faith was more a vision than an institution. They need what they have always needed: They need Christian community, not patriarchal clericalism. They need the sacred, not the sexist. The people need more prophets, not more priests. They need discipleship, not canonical decrees.

So what is to be done at a time like this when what is sought and what is possible are two different things? To what are we to give our energy when we are told no energy is wanted? The questions may sound new but the answer is an old one, an ancient one, a true one. The answer is discipleship.

The temptation is to become weary in the apparently fruitless search for office. The call is to become recommitted to the essential, the ancient, the authentic demands of discipleship. But Christian discipleship is a very dangerous thing. It has put every person who ever accepted it at risk. It made every follower who ever took it seriously on alert for rejection, from Martin of Tours to John Henry Newman, from Mary Ward to Dorothy Day.

Discipleship cast every fragile new Christian community in tension with the times in which it grew. To be a Christian community meant to defy Roman imperialism, to stretch Judaism, to counter pagan values with Christian ones. It demanded very concrete presence; it took great courage, unending fortitude, and clear public posture.

Real discipleship meant the rejection of emperor worship, the foreswearing of animal sacrifice, the inclusion of Gentiles, the elimination of dietary laws, the disavowal of circumcision, the acceptance of women, and the supplanting of law with love, of nationalism with universalism. Then, the following of Christ was not an excursion into the intellectual, the philosophical, the airy-fairy. It was not an arm-wrestling match with a tradition that was more history warped by culture than it was the spirit free of the system. It was real and immediate and cosmic.

The problem with Christian discipleship is that instead of simply requiring a kind of academic or ascetic exercise—the implication of most kinds of discipleship—Christian discipleship requires a kind of living that is sure, eventually, to tumble a person from the banquet tables of prestigious boards and the reviewing stands of presidents, and the processions of ecclesiastical knighthood to the most suspect margins of both church and society.

To follow Jesus, in other words, is to follow the one who turns the world upside down, even the religious world. It is a tipsy arrangement at the very least. People with high need for approval, social status, and public respectability need not apply. "Following Jesus" is a circuitous route that leads always and everywhere to places where a "nice" person would not go, to moments of integrity we would so much rather do without.

The Christian carries a worldview that cries for fulfillment now. Christian discipleship is not preparation for the hereafter or an ecstatic distance from the present. Christian discipleship is the commitment to live a certain way now. To follow Christ is to set about fashioning a world where the standards into which we have been formed become the standards, we too often find, we must ultimately foreswear. Flag and fatherland, profit and power, chauvinism and sexism, clericalism and authoritarianism done in the name of Christ are not Christian virtues, whatever the system that looks to them for legitimacy.

Christian discipleship is about living in this world the way that Christ lived in his—touching lepers, raising donkeys from ditches on Sabbath days, questioning the unquestionable, and consorting with women.

Discipleship implies a commitment to leave nets and homes, positions and securities, lordship and legalities to be now, in our own world, what Christ was for his: healer and prophet, voice and heart, call and sign of the God whose design for this world is justice and love. The disciple hears the poor, and ministers to the Hagars of this world who, having been used up by the establishment, are then abandoned to find their way alone, unaccompanied through a patriarchal world, unnoticed in a patriarchal world, unwanted in a patriarchal world but mightily, mightily patronized in a patriarchal world.

Discipleship is prepared to fly in the face of a world bent only on maintaining its own ends whatever the cost. The price is a high one. Teresa of Avila, John of the Cross, and Joan of Arc were persecuted for opposing the hierarchy itself—and then, later, canonized. Discipleship cost Mary Ward her health, her reputation, and even a Catholic burial. Discipleship cost Martin Luther King Jr. his life.

To the real disciple, to the true disciple the problem is clear: The church must not only preach the gospel, but it must not obstruct it. It must be what it says. It must demonstrate what it teaches. It must be judged by its own standards. Religion that colludes with the dispossession of the poor or the enslavement of the other in the name of patriotism becomes just one more instrument of the state. Religion that blesses oppressive governments in the name of obedience to an authority that denies the authority of conscience makes itself an oppressor as well. Religion that goes mute in the face of massive militarization practiced in the name of national defense abandons the God of love for the preservation of the civil religion. Religion that preaches the equality of women but does nothing to demonstrate it within its own structures, that proclaims an ontology of equality but insists on an ecclesiology of superiority is out of sync with its best self and dangerously close to repeating the theological errors that underlie centuries of church-sanctioned slavery.

The pauperization of women in the name of the sanctity and essentialism of motherhood flies in the face of the Jesus who overturned tables in the temple, contended with Pilate in the palace, chastised Peter to put away his sword and, despite the teaching of the day, cured the woman with the issue of blood and refused to allow his own apostles to silence the Samaritan woman on whose account, scripture tells us, "thousands believed that day."

Indeed, Jesus shows us, when women lack jurisdiction, church commissions lack women, and even altar girls are barred in a Christian community that says they are permitted, the invisibility of women in the church threatens the very nature of the church.

Obviously discipleship is not based on sexism, on civil quietism, or on private piety. On the contrary, discipleship confounds the "right reason" and "good sense" of patriarchy with right relationships and good heart. It pits the holy against the human. It pits the heart of Christ against the heartlessness of an eminently male-oriented, male-defined, male-controlled world. To be a disciple in the model of Judith and Esther, of Deborah and Ruth, of Mary and Mary Magdalene means to find ourselves forgers of a world where the weak confound the strong.

The disciple begins like the prophet Ruth to seek a world where the rich and the poor change places. The disciple sets out like the judge Deborah to shape a world where the last are made first and the first are last, starting with themselves. The disciple insists, as Jesus did, as the commander Judith did, on a world where women do what heretofore has been acceptable only for men simply because men said so. To the disciple who follows in the shadow of Esther, the savior of her people, the reign of God—the welcome of the outcast, the reverence of the other, the respect for creation—becomes a foreign land made home. "Come follow me" becomes an anthem of public proclamation from which no one, no one, is excluded and for which no risk is too great.

Discipleship, we know from the life of the Christ whom we follow, is not membership in a clerical social club called a church. That is not an ordination that the truly ordained can abide. Discipleship is not an intellectual exercise of assent to a body of doctrine. Discipleship is an attitude of mind, a quality of soul, a way of living that is not political but which has serious political implications, that may not be officially ecclesiastical but which changes the church that is more ecclesiastical than communal. Discipleship changes things because it simply cannot ignore things as they are; it refuses anything and everything that defies the will of God for humanity, no matter how sensible, no matter how reasonable, no matter how common, no matter how obvious, no matter how historically patriarchal, no matter how often it has been called "the will of God" by those who purport to determine what that is.

The disciple takes public issue with the values of a world that advantages only those who are already advantaged. The disciple takes aim at institutions that call themselves "freeing" but which keep half the people of the world in bondage; they take umbrage at systems that are more bent on keeping "those kind of people"— improper people, that is—out of them than they are in welcoming all people into them.

True discipleship takes the side always, always, always of the poor despite the power of the rich—not because the poor are more virtuous than the rich but because the God of love wills for them what the rich ignore for them. Discipleship cuts a reckless path through corporation types like Herod, through institution types like the Pharisees, through system types like the money-changers, and through chauvinist types like apostles who want to send women away.

Discipleship stands bare naked in the middle of the world's marketplace and, in the name of Jesus, cries aloud all the cries of the world until someone, somewhere hears and responds to the poorest of the poor, the lowest of the low, the most outcast of the rejected. Anything else—all the pomp, all the gold lace and red silk, all the rituals in the world—the gospels attest, is certainly mediocre and surely bogus discipleship.

It is one thing, then, for an individual to summon the courage it takes to stand alone in the eye of a storm called "the real world." It is another thing entirely to see the church itself be anything less than the living Christ. Why? Because the church of Jesus Christ is not called to priesthood, the church of Christ is called to discipleship.

To see a church of Christ deny the poor and the outcast their due, institute the very systems in itself that it despises in society, is to see no church at all. It is at best religion reduced to one more social institution designed to comfort the comfortable but not to challenge the chains that bind most of humanity—all of its women—to the cross. In this kind of church, the gospel has been long reduced to the catechism. In this kind of church, prophecy dies and justice whimpers and the truth becomes too dim for the searching to see. Today, as never before in history, perhaps, the world and therefore the church within it, is being stretched to the breaking point by life situations that, if for no other reason than their immensity, are shaking the globe at its foundations.

New life questions emerge with startling impact and relentless persistence. And the greatest of them all is the woman's question. Women are most of the poor, most of the refugees, most of the uneducated, most of the beaten, most of the rejected of the world. In the church, educated, dedicated, committed women are ignored even in the pronouns of the Mass. Where is the presence of Jesus to the homeless woman, to the beggar woman, to the abandoned woman, to the woman alone, to the woman whose questions, cries, and life experience have no place in the systems of the world and no place in the church either? Except, of course, to be defined as a second kind of human nature, not quite as competent, not quite as valued, not quite as human, not quite as graced by God as men?

What does the theology of discipleship demand here? What does the theology of a priestly people imply here? Are women simply half a disciple of Christ? To be half commissioned, half noticed, and half valued?

In the light of these situations, there are, consequently, questions in the Christian community today that cannot be massaged by footnotes nor obscured by jargon nor made palatable by the retreat to "faith." On the contrary, before these issues, the footnotes falter, the language serves only to heighten the question, faith itself demands the question. The discipleship of women is the question that is not going to go away. Indeed, the discipleship of the church in regard to women is the question that will, in the long run, prove the church itself.

In the woman's question the church is facing one of its most serious challenges to discipleship since the emergence of the slavery question when we argued, too, that slavery was the will of God. The major question facing Christians today, perhaps, is, What does discipleship mean in a church that doesn't want women? If discipleship is reduced to maleness, what does that do to the rest of the Christian dispensation? If only men can really live discipleship to the fullest, what is the use of a woman aspiring to discipleship at all? What does it mean for the women themselves who are faced with rejection, devaluation, and a debatable theology based on the remnants of a bad biology theologized? What do we do when a church proclaims the equality of women but builds itself on structures that assure their inequality?

What, as well, does the rejection of women at the highest levels of the church mean for men who claim to be enlightened but continue to support the very system that mocks half the human race? What does it mean for the church that claims to be a follower of the Jesus who pulled asses out of ditches on the Sabbath and raised women from the dead and contended with the teachers of the faith—*mandatum* or no *mandatum*, definitive documents or no definitive documents? And finally what does it mean for a society badly in need of a cosmic worldview on the morning of a global age?

The answers are discouragingly clear on all counts. Christian discipleship is not simply in danger of being stunted. Discipleship has, in fact, become the enemy. Who we do not want to admit to full, official, legitimated discipleship—something the church itself teaches is required of us all—has become at least as problematic for the integrity of the church as the people who continue to exclude women from the offices of the church that shape its theology and minister to its people.

Women are beginning to wonder if discipleship has anything to do with them at all. And therein lies the contemporary question of discipleship. Some consider faithfulness to the gospel to mean doing what we have always done. Others find faithfulness only in being what we have always been. The distinction is crucial. The distinction is also essential to the understanding of discipleship in the modern church. When "the tradition" becomes synonymous with "the system" and maintaining the system becomes more important than maintaining the spirit of the tradition, discipleship shrivels and becomes at best "obedience" or "fidelity" to the past but not deep-down commitment to the presence of the living Christ confronting the leprosies of the age.

Discipleship presumes from each of us, from the church itself, that same kind of reckless, open, receiving, giving love that Jesus brought to the blind on the roads of Galilee, to the body of a dead girl, to the plea of the woman with the issue of blood.

Society called the blind sinful, a female child useless, a menstruating woman unclean, all of them marginal to the system, condemned to the fringes of life, excluded from the center of the synagogue, barred from the heart of the temple. But Jesus takes each of them to himself, despite the laws, regardless of the culture, notwithstanding the disapproval of the spiritual notables of the area and fills them with himself and sends them as himself out to the highways and byways of the entire world.

To be disciples of Jesus means that we must do the same. There are some things, it seems, that brook no rationalizing for the sake of institutional niceties. Discipleship infers, implies, requires no less than the confirming, ordaining love of Jesus for everyone, everywhere regardless of who would dare to take upon themselves the audacious right to draw limits around the love of God. Discipleship and faith are of a piece. To say that we believe that God loves the poor, judges in their behalf, wills their deliverance but do nothing ourselves to free the poor, to hear their pleas, to lift their burdens, to act in their behalf is an empty faith indeed. To say that God is love and not ourselves love as God loves may well be church but it is not Christianity.

To proclaim a theology of equality, to say that all persons are equal in God's sight and at the same time to maintain a theology of inequality, a spirituality of domination in the name of God that says that women have no place in the dominion of the church and the development of doctrine is to live a lie.

But if discipleship is the following of Jesus, beyond all bounds, at all costs, for the bringing of the reign of God, for the establishment of right relationships, then to ground a woman's calling to follow Christ in her ability to look like Jesus obstructs the very thing the church is founded to do. It obstructs a woman's ability to follow Christ to the full, to give her life for the others, to bless and preach and sacrifice and build community "in His name"—as the documents on priesthood say that a priestly people must. And it does it for the sake of religion and in defiance of the gospel itself. How can a church such as this call convincingly to the world in the name of justice to practice a justice it does not practice itself?

How is it that the church can call other institutions to deal with women as full human beings made in the image of God when their humanity is precisely what the church itself holds against them in the name of God? It is a philosophical question of immense proportions. It is the question which, like slavery, brings the church to the test. For the church to be present to the woman's question, to minister to it, to be disciple to it, the church must itself become converted to the issue. In fact, the church must become converted by the issue.

Men who do not take the woman's issue seriously may be priests but they cannot possibly be disciples. They cannot possibly be other Christs, not the Christ born of a woman. Not the Christ who commissioned women to preach him. Not the Christ who took faculties from a woman at Cana. Not the Christ who sent women to preach resurrection to apostles who would not believe it. Not the Christ who sent the Holy Spirit on Mary the woman as well as on Peter the man. Not the Christ who announced his messiahship as clearly to the Samaritan woman as to the Rock that shattered. If this is the Jesus whom we as Christians, as church, are to follow, then the discipleship of the church is now mightily in question.

Indeed, the poet Basho writes: "I do not seek to follow in the footsteps of those of old. I seek the things they sought."

Discipleship depends on our bringing the will of God for humankind to the questions of this age as Jesus did to his. As long as tradition is used to mean following in the footsteps of our past rather than seeking to maintain the spirit of the Christ in the present, then it is unlikely that we will preserve more than the shell of the church. The consciousness of the universalism of humanity across differences has become the thread that binds the world together in a global age. What was once a hierarchy of humankind is coming to be seen for what it is: the oppression of humankind.

To most of the world, the colonization of women is as unacceptable now as the colonial oppression of Africa, the crusades against Turks, the enslavement of blacks, and the decimation of Indians in the name of God. In Asia, Buddhist women are demanding ordination and the right to make the sacred mandalas. In India, women are beginning to do the sacred dances and light the sacred fires. In Judaism, women study Torah and carry the scrolls and read the scriptures and lead the congregations. Only in the most backward, most legalistic, most primitive of cultures are women made invisible, made useless, made less than fully human, less than fully spiritual.

The humanization of the human race is upon us. The only question for the church is whether the humanization of the human race will lead as well to the Christianization of the Christian church. Otherwise, discipleship will die and the integrity of the church with it.

We must take discipleship seriously or we shall leave the church of the future with functionaries but without disciples. The fact is that Christianity lives in Christians, not in books, not in documents called "definitive" to hide the fact that they are at best time-bound. Not in platitudes about "special vocations," not in old errors dignified as "tradition."

The new fact of life is that discipleship to women and the discipleship of women are key to the discipleship of the rest of the church. The questions are clear. The answer is obscure and uncertain but crucial to the future of a church that claims to be eternal.

A priestly people in a priestless period must keep the total vision clearly in mind. But we must also keep the tasks of the present clearly in hand, and the task of the present is not preparation for ordination in a church that either doubts, or fears, the power of the truth to persuade and so denies the right to discuss the festering question of whether or not women can participate in the sacrament of orders. That would be premature, at best, if not downright damaging.

No, the task of the present in a time such as this is to use every organization to which we belong to develop the theology of the church to a point of critical mass.

We need a group free of *mandatums* that will organize seminars, hold public debates in the style of the great medieval disputations on the full humanity of Indians, hold teach-ins, sponsor publications, write books, post Web sites, and gather discussion groups around the topics of the infallibility of infallibility and the *sensus fidelium*.

The task of the present is surely for groups like this to question the clear exclusion of women from the restoration of the permanent diaconate, an official manner of discipleship that has theology, history, ritual, liturgy, and tradition firmly, fully and clearly on its side. It's time to bring into the light of day the discussions that lurk behind every church door, in every seeking heart.

If as Vatican II says, priesthood requires preaching, sacrifice, and community building, then the preaching, shaping, and vision of a new notion of priest and deacon—whatever the cost to ourselves—may be the greatest priestly service of them all right now. So we must keep turning, turning, turning in the direction of discipleship, as women always have. But differently. For as Basho says, we do not seek to follow in the footsteps of those of old. We seek the things they sought. We don't seek to do what they really need. We need much more than that. We need now to do what they really, really need.

# Conversion

⟶

"It is good to have an end to journey towards," Ursula Le Guin writes, "but it is the journey that matters in the end." The truth of that statement explains, as well as anything, I think, how it is possible, necessary even, for me as a Roman Catholic to stay in a church that is riddled with inconsistencies, closed to discussion about the implications of them, and sympathetic only to invisible women. The fact is that I have come to realize over the years that church is not a place, it is a process. To leave the church may, in fact, be leaving part of the process of my own development. And so, intent on the process of grappling with truth, I stay in it when, for a woman, staying in it is full of pain, frustration, disillusionment, and far too often, even humiliation. Both of us, this church and I, have need to grow. The church needs to grow in its understanding of the gospel, and I need to grow in my understanding of myself as I strive to live it. It is, in other words, a journey of conversion for both of us.

There is, moreover, a model for the staying that lurks within me, prodding me in hard times to trust my questions, accusing me on dark days of prizing weakness more than truth, consoling me in hard times with the courage of endurance, and inspiring me always to maintain the faith whatever the weakness of the system that heralds it. The images that haunt me are the memories of Jesus contesting with the Pharisees, Jesus weeping over Jerusalem, Jesus teaching in the synagogue, and Jesus presiding over the Seder on Holy Thursday. My models are clear: they are Jesus proclaiming his truth whatever the situation, whatever the cost; Jesus grappling with the depression that comes from failure, from rejection; Jesus trusting the truth, living the faith, and hoping to the end.

Those are the models that make the rest of the journey—its purpose, its value—clear to me. Staying in the church even when the church has little time for women's presence, takes little notice of women's questions, holds little respect for women's insights, devotes itself to preaching the gospel of equality for women but preserves a male theology and a male system, this demands a purpose far beyond ourselves.

I stay in the church, a restless pilgrim, not because I don't believe what the church has taught me but precisely because I do. I believed when they taught us that God made us equal and Jesus came for us all. I believed in the Jesus they showed me who listened to women and taught theology to women and sent women to teach theology and raised women from the dead. And so today, I believe that the church, if it is ever to be true to that same gospel, must someday do the same—it must commission women as Jesus did the Samaritan woman, listen to women as Jesus did the Caananite women, raise women to new life as Jesus did the daughter of Jairus. I stay in the church because there is nowhere else I know that satisfies in me what the church itself teaches us to seek: a sacramental life that makes all life sacred, a community of faith that celebrates life together, the proclamation of the image of God alive in each of us, the contemplation of truth that makes life meaningful. I know clubs and societies and congregations of deep sincerity who do great good. The problem is that I need sacrament and common faith and a sense of the divine in the core of my humanity as well as I need good talk, good works, and good intentions.

I stay in the church because, though the lights have gone out in parts of the house, I know myself to be at home. I realize now with penetrating anger how sexist the church itself really is, whatever its professions of faith in Jesus and love for women. But I also realize that this is the family I was raised in. This is the family that gave me my first images of God, my first feeling of human worth, my first sense of holiness, my first invitation to a goodness measured by more than "success." Just because a family is dysfunctional, as this one is, does not make it less the family. If anything, we must work all the harder to bring all of us to health in it.

I stay in the church because I have the support from other women, from feminist men, from a women's community that enables me to worship with human dignity and a sense of theological inclusion. Otherwise, I do not know how possible it would be to stay. At the same time, because I know my own need for the strength of a conscious and understanding community, I have come to understand and honor those who, lacking that kind of support, choose to leave it. For many, churchgoing has become more an experience of systemic devaluation than spiritual growth. After years of waiting for change, then, they have chosen to try to find God by themselves rather than being excluded by the community from the common search. These are the women in whom beats a Catholic heart but, like many another abused or belittled woman, they get to the point where, for their mental health, say with pain and still with love, "I will not divorce you but until this changes, I cannot live under the same roof."

I stay in the church for the simple reason that because it has come through so much already, I know it can come through more. This is the church that finally repented the Inquisition, that eventually accepted Galileo, that at length stopped selling relics, and that, in the end, caught up with Luther and at long last embraced an ecumenical movement. Among other things. This is a church that has known sin and regretted it. This is a church that has the potential, the credentials, to understand mine as well.

I stay in the church, wiser now, less idealistic, more balanced in my hope for instant change, more spiritually mature myself, perhaps. In the first two weeks of my initial trip to Rome in 1972, I was appalled by what I saw there—the pomp, the posturing, the oppressive and arrogant sense of power that seeped out of every office, hung over every meeting, colored every ritual. I was young and intense. I had, I thought, lost my faith. I wanted never to go back there. "*Patientia, patientia,*" an old monastic counseled. "You will come back and you will grow to understand. . . ." The sentence trailed off into irritating nothingness. Understand what? But by the end of the next two weeks and the next fifteen years of meetings there, I came to understand its meaning for myself. I grew to realize that for those whose faith is mature, only God is God. Not the institution. Not the system. Not the history. Not the pope. God is in the church, not in the chancery. The church is a vehicle for the faith, not the end of it.

Finally, I stay in the church because the sexist church I love needs women for its own salvation. The truth it holds, women test for authenticity.

We are sanctifying one another, this church and the women who refuse to be silent, refuse to be suppressed. What each of us sets out to convert will in the end convert us as well. Women will call the church to truth. The church will call women to faith. Together, God willing, we will persist, women despite the madness of authoritarianism, and the church regardless of the irritation of unrelenting challenge. We will perdure together. We will propel ourselves to the edges of our potentials for holiness.

"Why does a woman like you stay in the church?" a woman asked me from the depths of a dark audience years ago. "Because," I answered, "every time I thought about leaving, I found myself thinking of oysters." "Oysters?" she said. "What do oysters have to do with it?" "Well," I answered her in the darkness of the huge auditorium, "I realized that an oyster is an organism that defends itself by excreting a substance to protect itself against the sand of its spawning bed. The more sand in the oyster, the more chemical the oyster produces until finally, after layer upon layer of gel, the sand turns into a pearl. And the oyster itself becomes more valuable in the process. At that moment, I discovered the ministry of irritation."

I stay in the church with all my challenge and despite its resistance, knowing that before this is over, both it and I will have become what we have the capacity to be—followers of the Christ who listened to women, taught them theology, and raised them from the dead.

# *Acknowledgments*

⟲

BlueBridge and Benetvision gratefully acknowledge the following publications in which parts of this book previously appeared, as well as the following venues where parts of this book were previously given as speeches:

The chapter *Simplicity* appeared as "Simplicity of Life" in *Liguorian*, February 1995; the chapter *Work* appeared as "Work: My Share of the Life of God" in *Liguorian*, September 1993; the chapter *Sabbath* appeared as "Sins of the '90s: The Lost Sabbath" in *The Tablet*, March 1997; the chapter *Stewardship* was published as Chapter 5, "Monasticism," in *Christianity and Ecology*, edited by Elizabeth Breuilly and Martin Palmer © The Continuum International Publishing Group 1992 (reprinted with the permission of the publisher); the chapter *Contemplation* was an interview, "Contemplation, Everyone?," published in *Praying Magazine*, January-February 1991; the chapter *Prayer* appeared as "Monastic Prayer: Unchanging Change" in *Religious Life Review*, September-October 1998; the chapter *Empowerment* was a lecture, "Empowerment and Spirituality," given at the Future of the American Church Conference, Washington, DC, September 1989; the chapter *Prophecy* was the Guilfoil Memorial Lecture, "Thomas Merton: Seeder of Radical Action and the Enlightened Heart," given in Kansas City, MO, February 2001; the chapter *Wholeness* was a lecture, "Theology, Ecology and Feminism," given at the Episcopal Theological Seminary, Austin, TX, September 2003; the chapter *Sanctity* appeared as "Icons, Rebels, Stars and Saints: Holiness in the Catholic Tradition" in the SIDIC (Service International de Documentation Judéo-Chrétienne) Bulletin, July 1997; the chapter *Tradition* appeared as "The Justice Lessons Jesus Grew Up On" in *Salt*, September 1990; the chapter *Equality* appeared as "A Woman's Place" in *Notre Dame Magazine*, Winter 1991-92; the chapter *Ministry* was a lecture, "Ministry to a Wounded World," given at the Massachusetts Biblical Society Conference, Boston, MA, October 2003; the chapter *Vision* was the concluding address, "Both Roots and Wings: Moving the Vatican II Church Into a New Millennium," at the three 2001 Call to Action National Conferences held in Los Angeles, Philadelphia and Chicago; the chapter *Discipleship* was a presentation, "Discipleship for a Priestly People in a Priestless Period," given at the Women's Ordination Worldwide 1st International Conference in Dublin, Ireland, June 2001; the chapter *Conversion* appeared as "Why I Stay" in *Lutheran Woman Today*, October 1996.

Some of the writings were slightly edited for this book.